East L.A. Barrio Codex

A Journey into Asemic and Codex Writing

by
Israel F.
Haros
Lopez

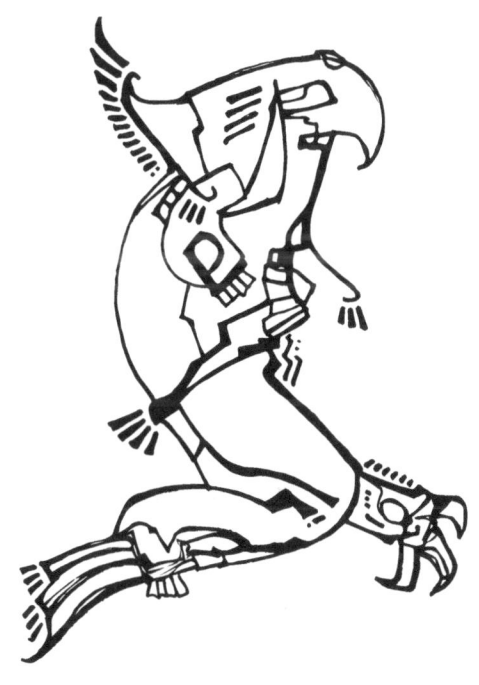

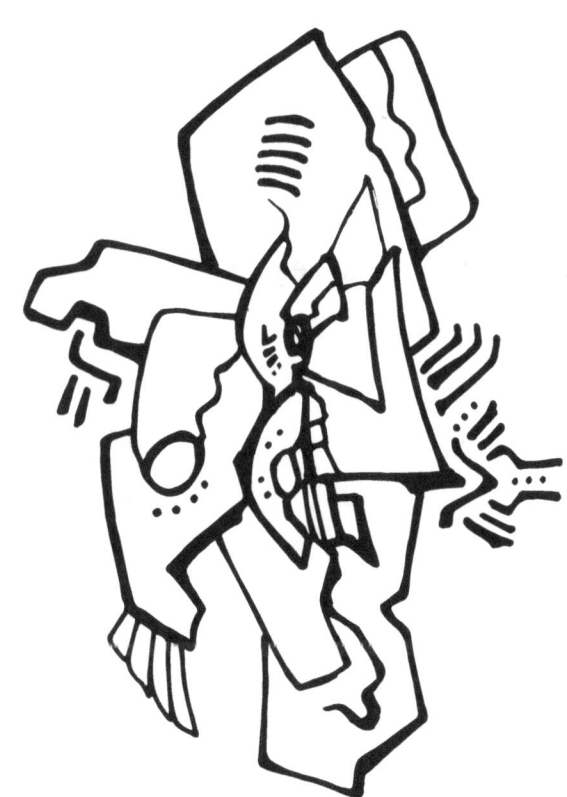

East L.A. Barrio Codex:
A Journey Into Asemic and Codex Writing

First Edition
Illustrated by Israel F. Haros Lopez

Cover Design by
Israel F. Haros Lopez

East L.A. Barrio Codex: A Journey Into Asemic and Codex Writing

Published by Waterhummingbirdhouse Press
Library of Congress Catologing-in-Publication Data is available upon request

ISBN-13:
978-1502394347

ISBN-10:
1502394340

dedicated to all the barrio street artists
especially those that have died, been arrested,
locked up in the struggle for artistic expression
for all those who have managed to create and be free in this form
for all those that have inspired us with their creativity in the neighborhoods
all the muralists. all those that continue to inspire with art straight from the source.

dedicated to Michael Jacobson and all the asemic writers of the world
trying to find a language beyond where we are for all those trying to deconstruct and
construct at another form of communication. Thank You Michael for taking the time to
archive and publish others works. Thank you for your craft and dedication and honoring
the work of others

This work is an experiment in language searching back to ancestral truths, being
present in the now and searching towards seven generations forward. it was made
entirely using black permanent markers. The images were then scanned and
vectorized. This work is part of a culmination of work that has probing, questioning,
investigating mayan, tolteca, azteca, olmeca language over the last 12 or so years.
While it draws from the iconograpy its my attempt to break away and continue the
conversation from my heart's perspective. Moving and experimenting in ways before i
had a name for what i was doing. So grateful for Jesús Aldana-Alba for leading me to
Michael Jacobson's work and the work of other asemic writers. Sometimes its good to
have labels and know that there are others out there pursuing similar inquiries. The
feeling of 'you are not alone' creates multitude of inspiration to work long days and
nights alone investigating. probing. pushing forward alone. So Thank you to all you
experimenting and taking the work so serious. And thank you to those that this is a
bunch of jibberish. You help the ego and the pride as we push forward in our
investigations of the self, of the future of lenguaje, abstraction and orienting ourselves in
making sense of the current world madness.

And of course to my beautiful Isabel that mirrors me, laughs and cries with me, sees me
working like a monkey and supports me and joins me in creating weapons of mass
creation. Thank you for listening and understanding me even when we are in silence.
Even when you are just observing and caring and loving me. You inspire me and allow
me to be freer. Tlazokamati mi amore.

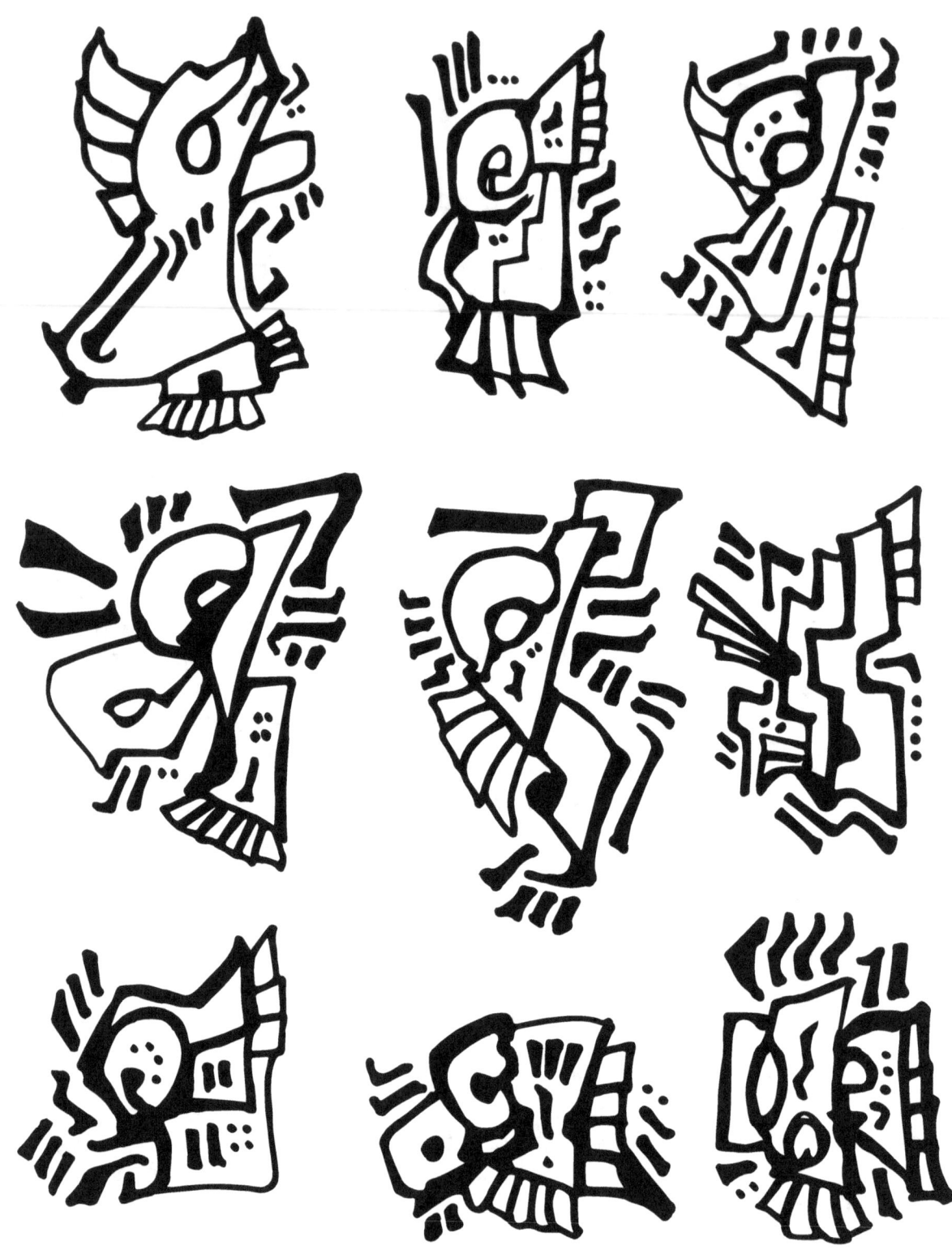

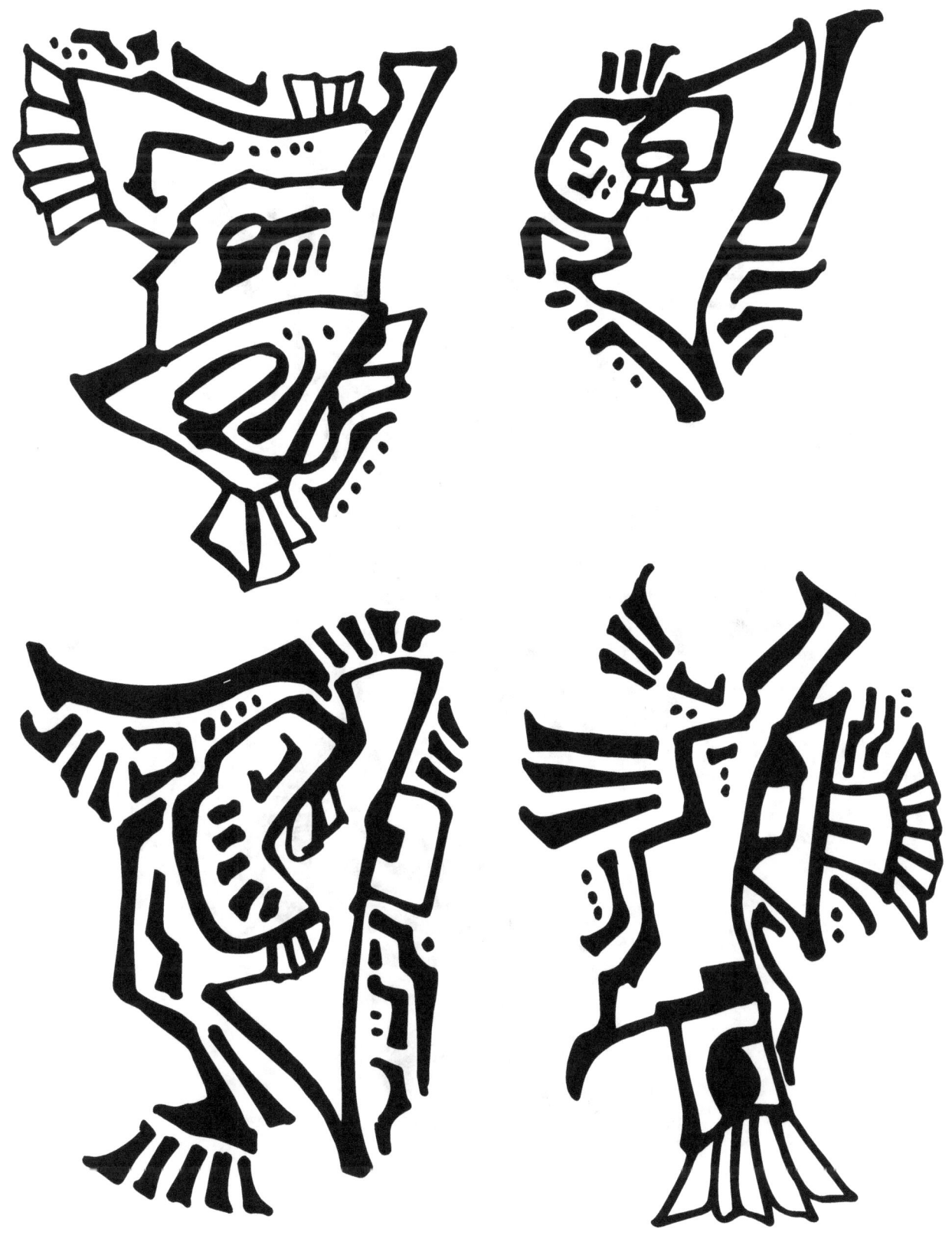

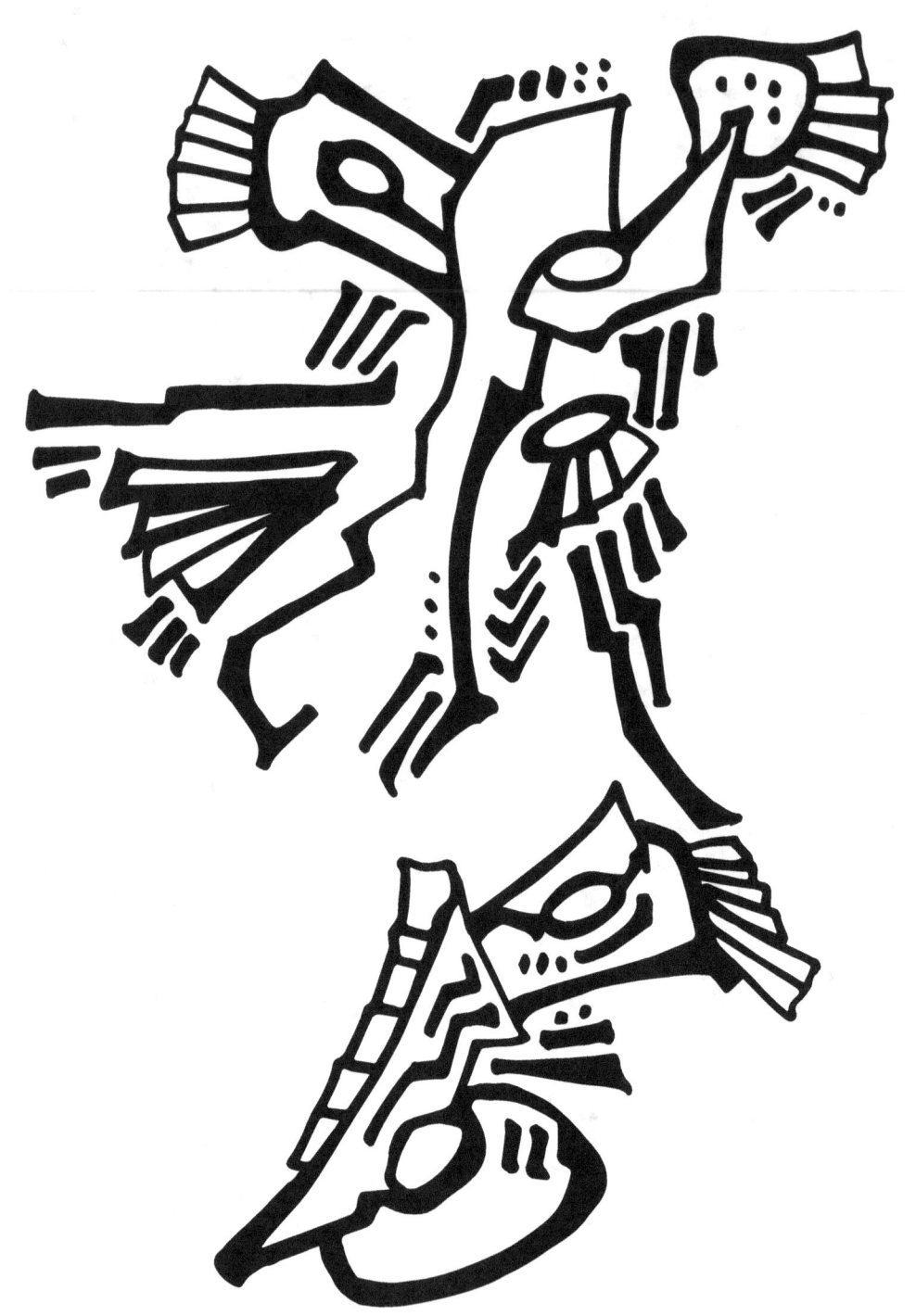

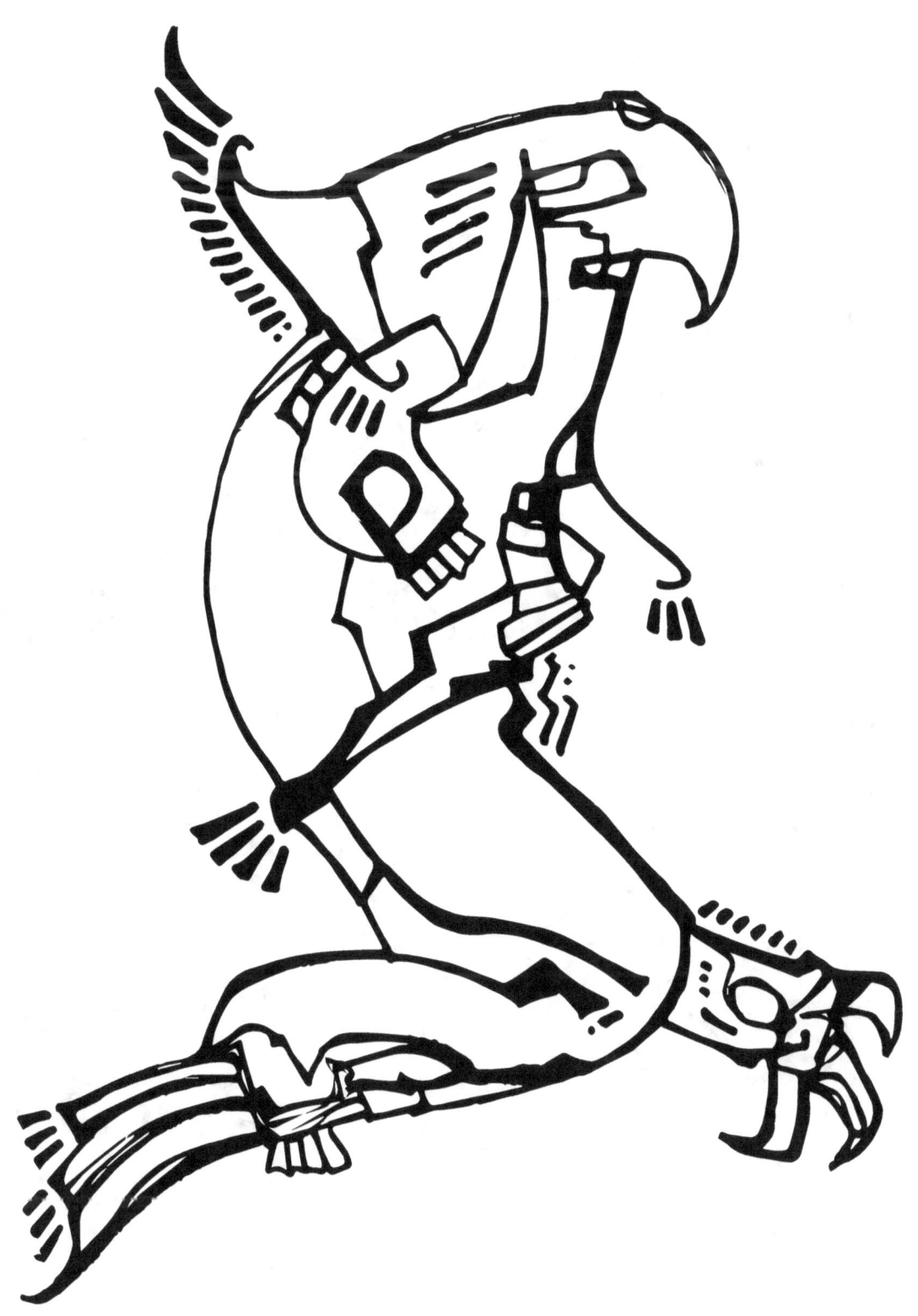

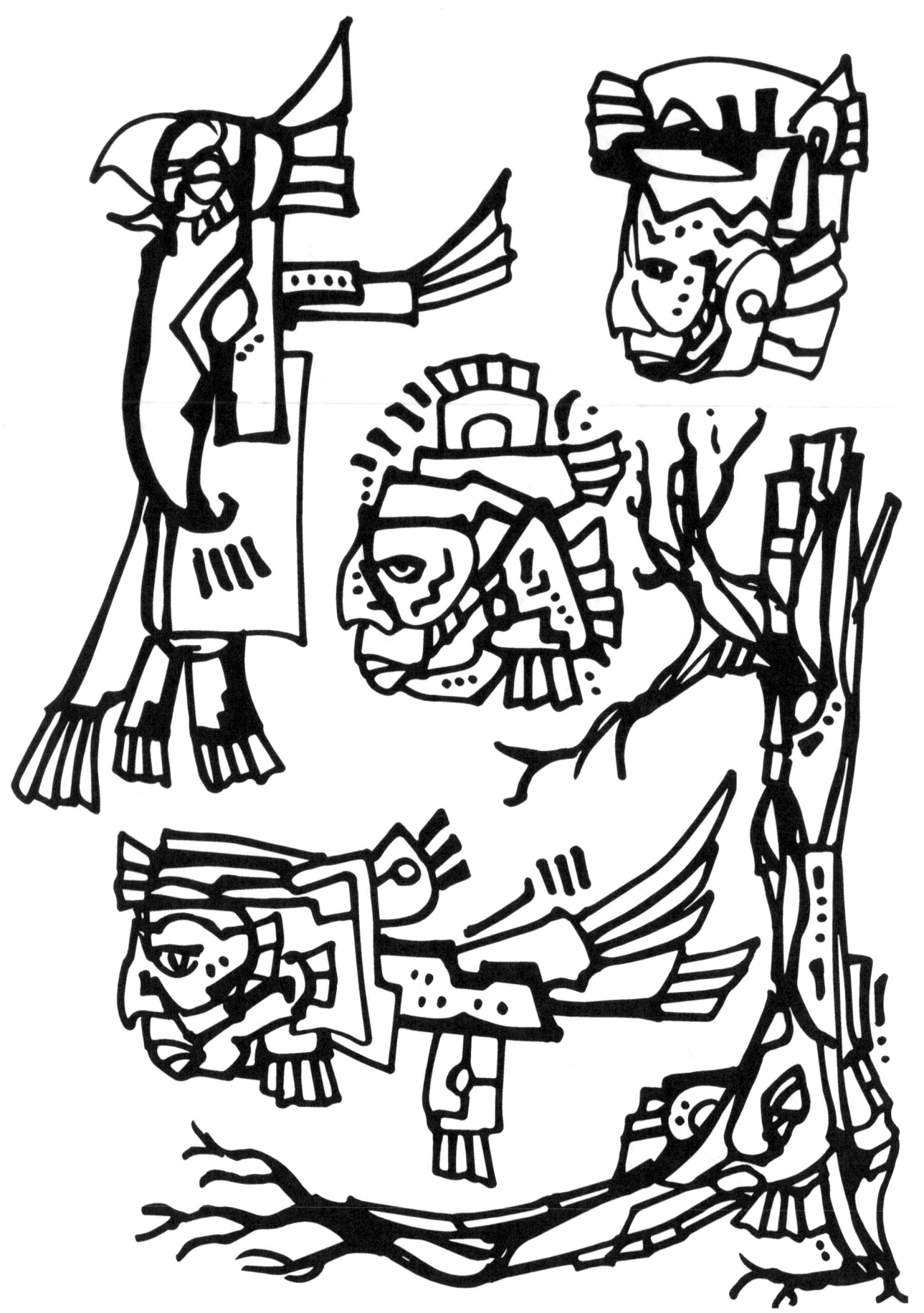

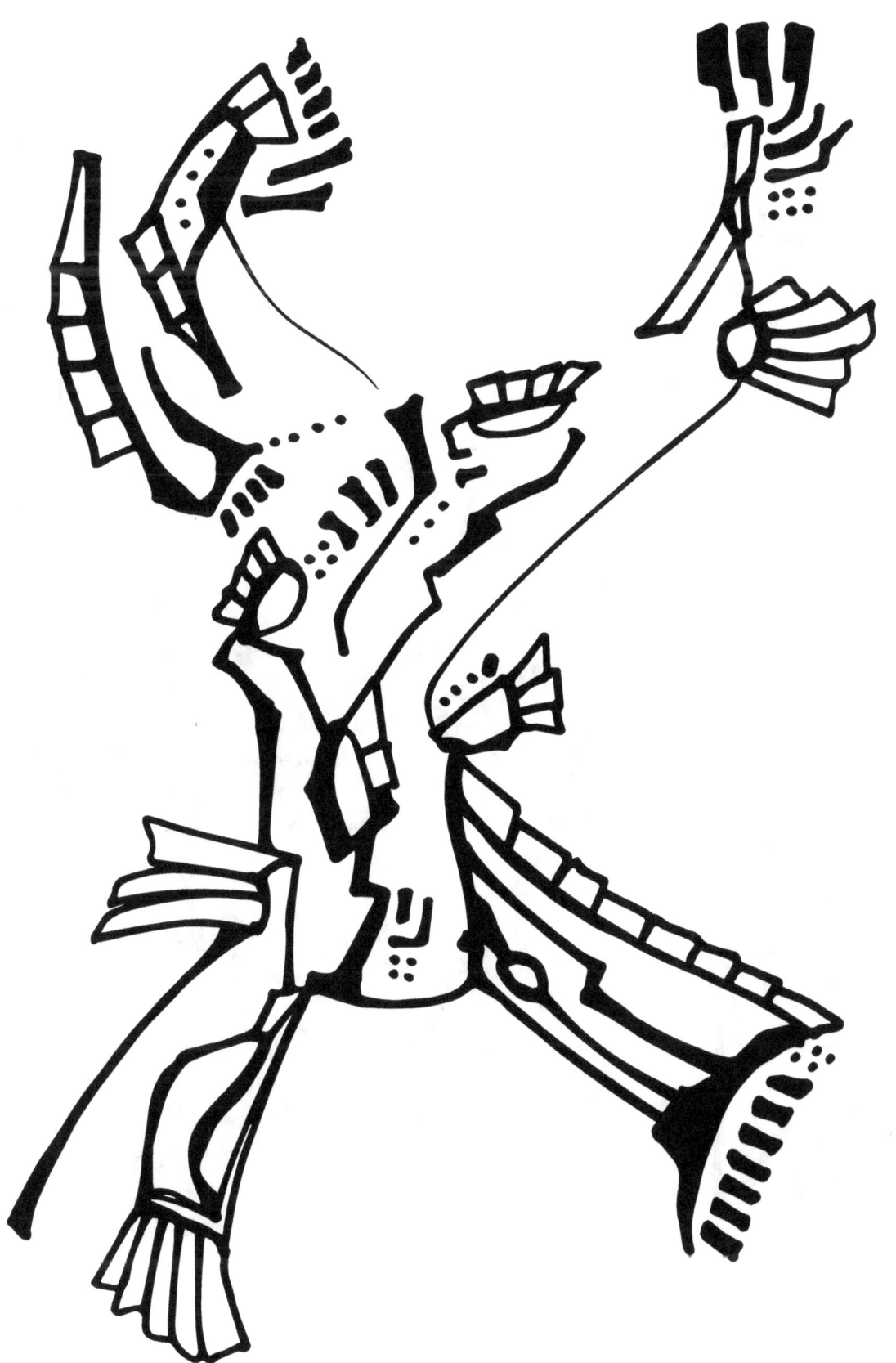

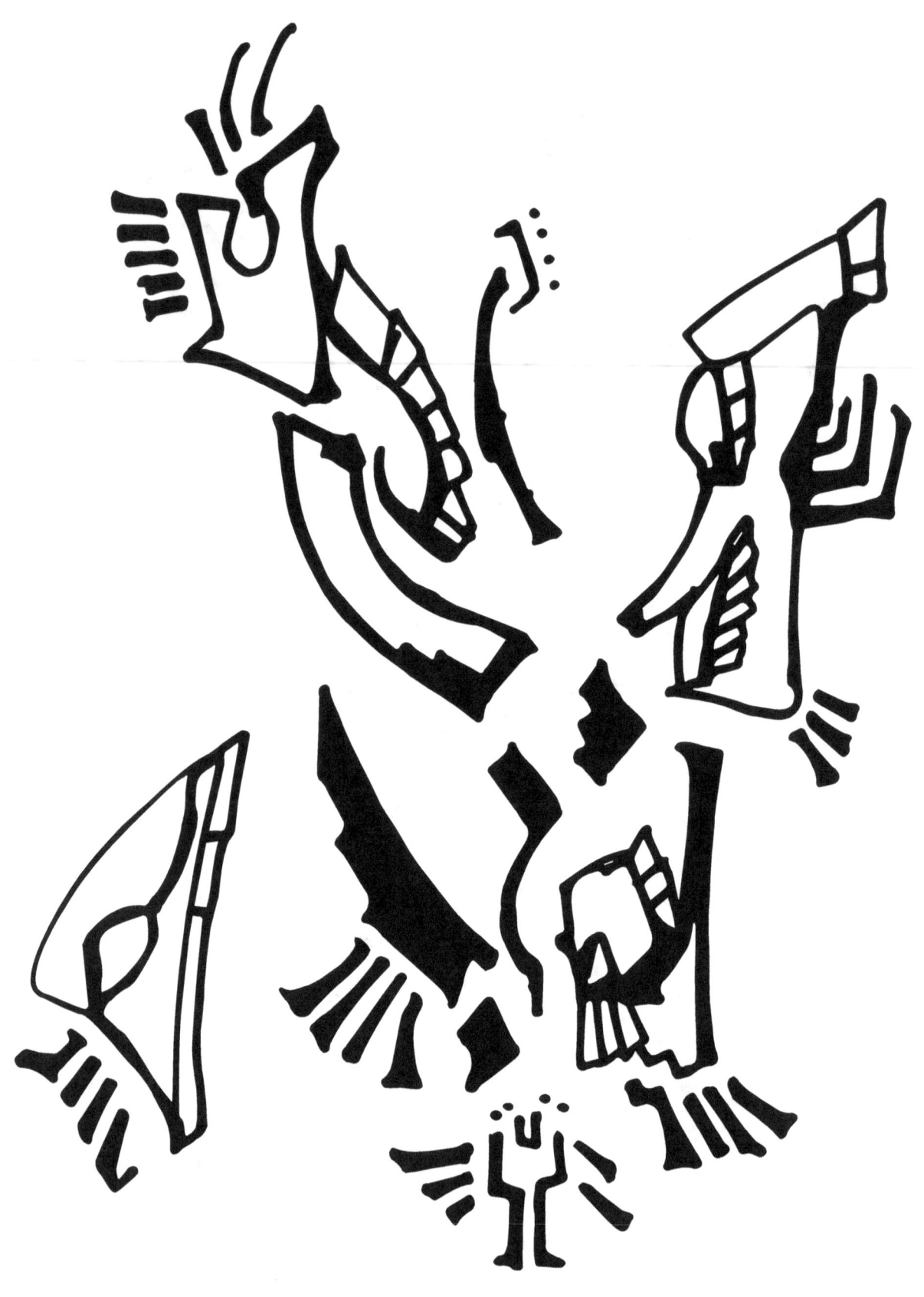

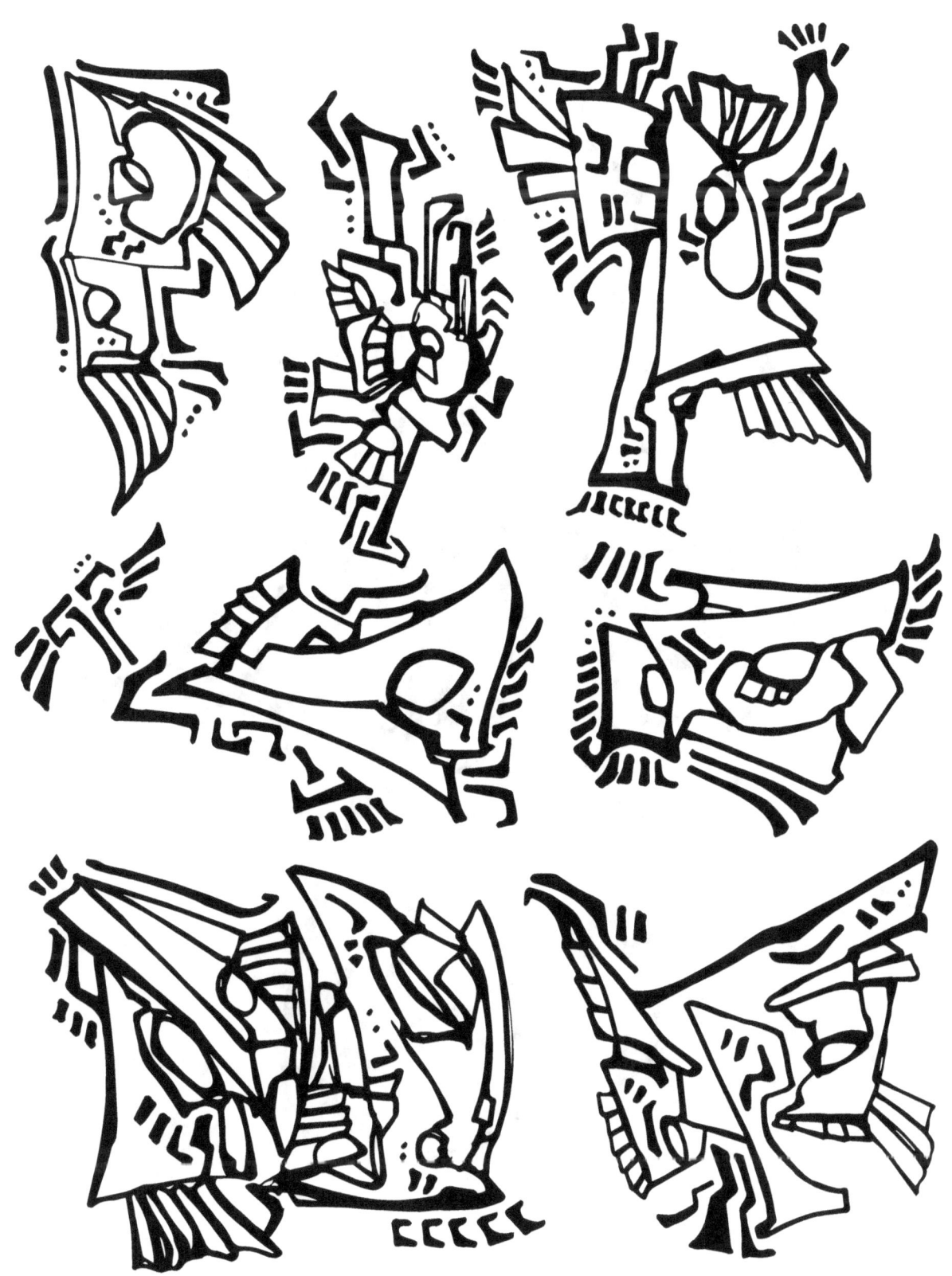

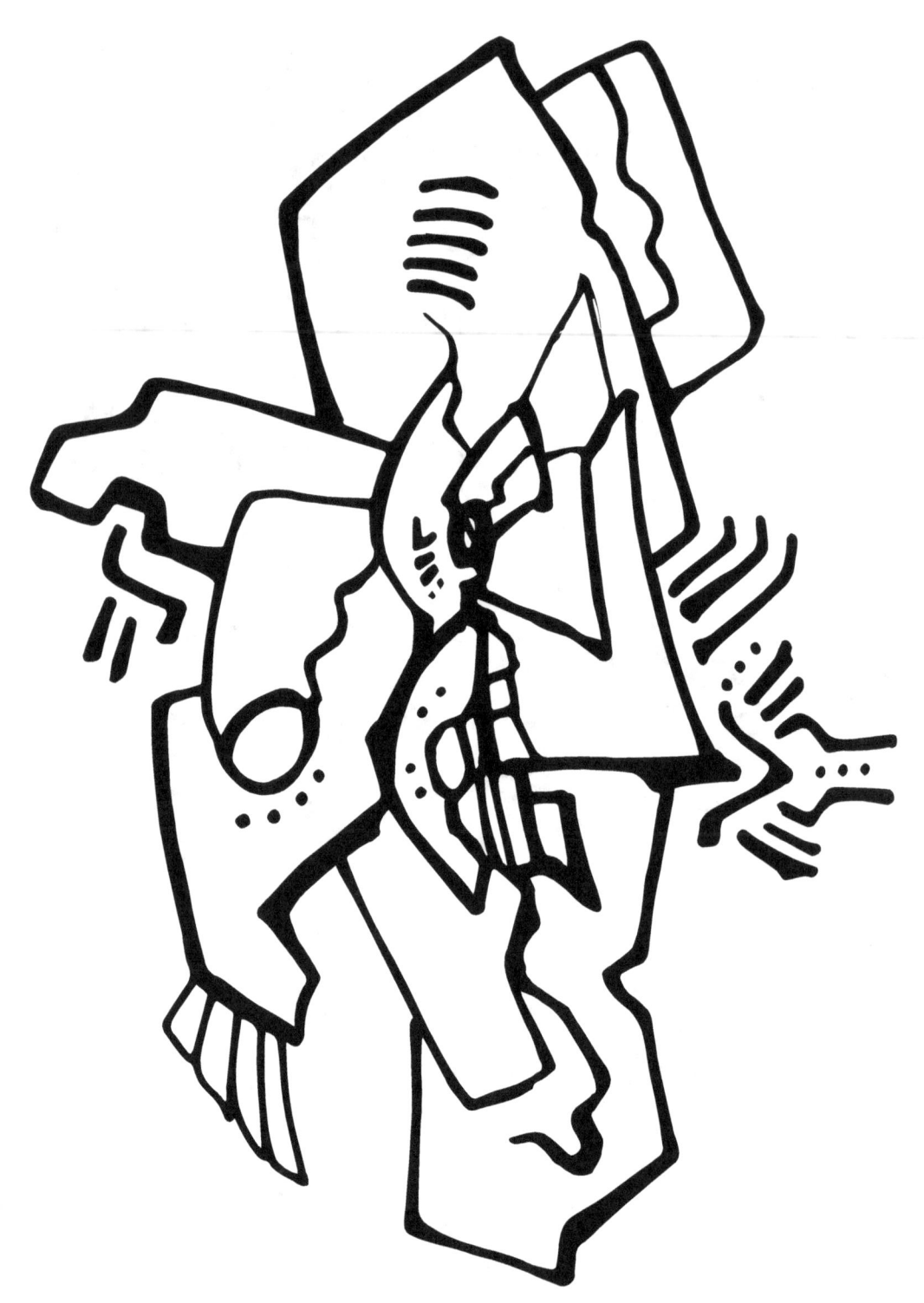

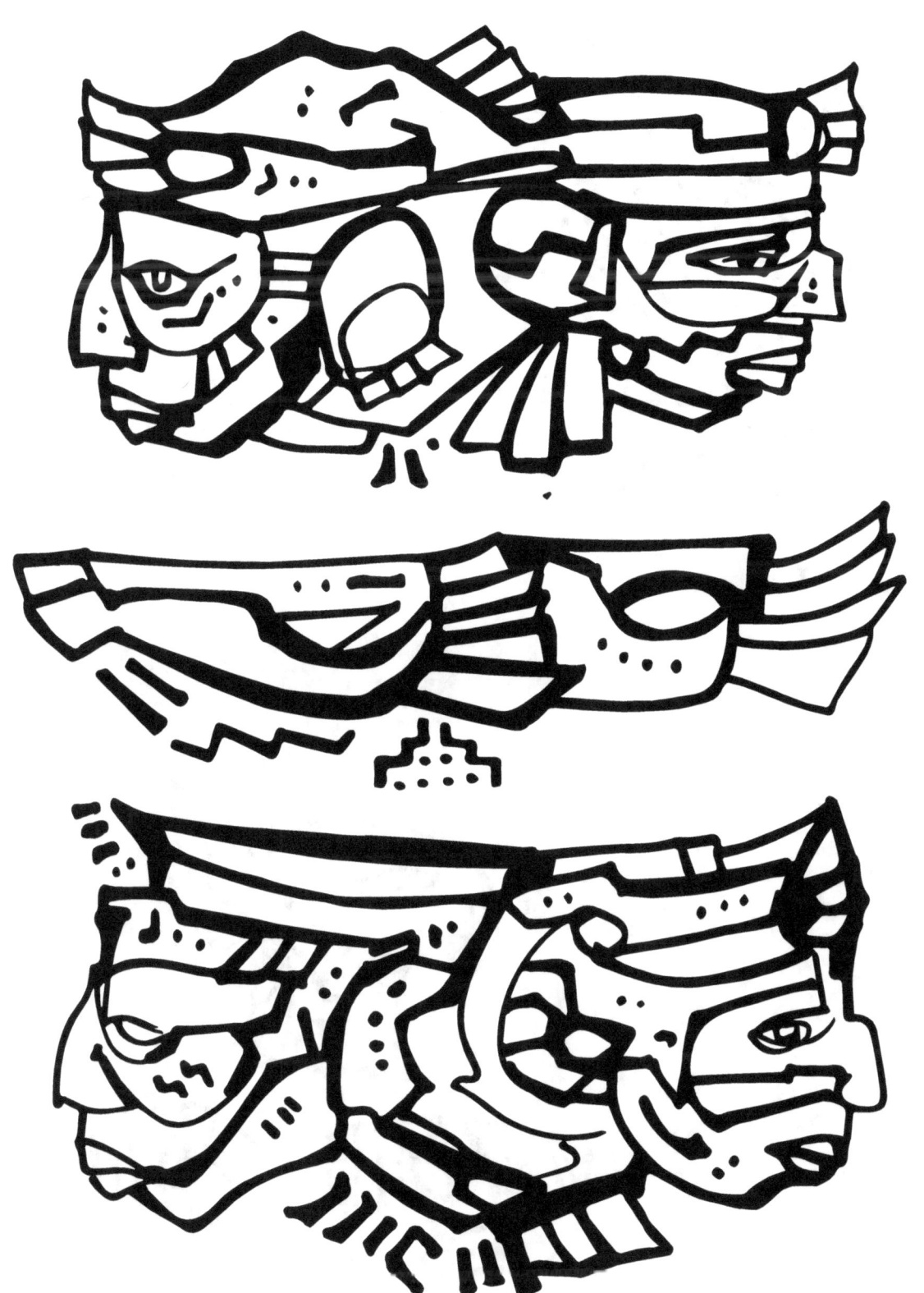

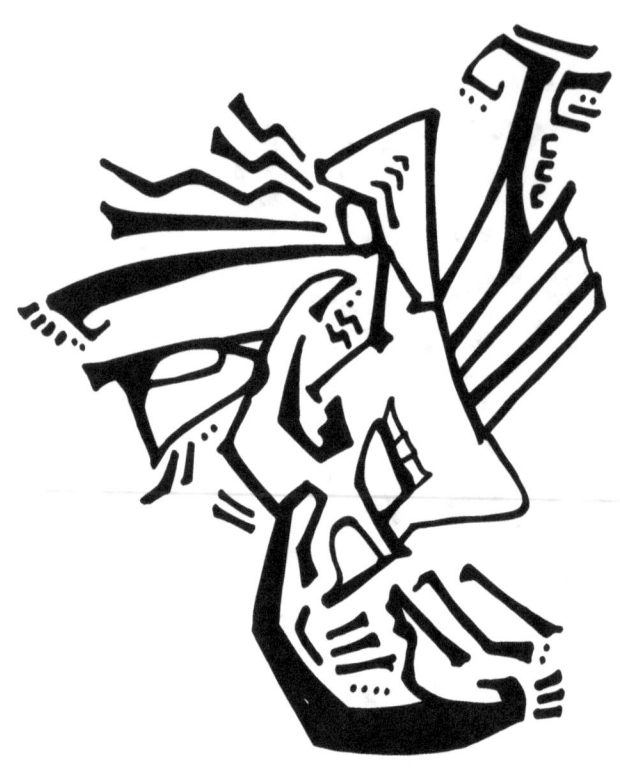

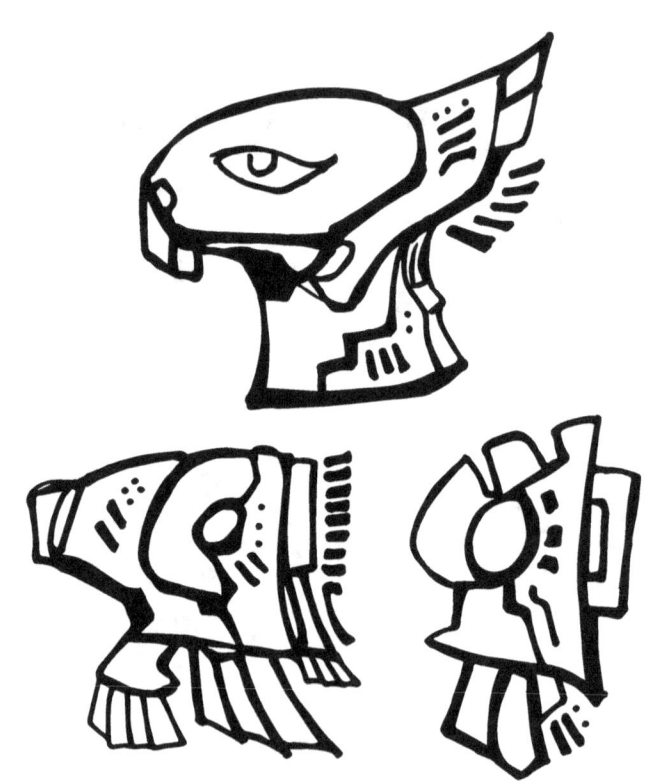

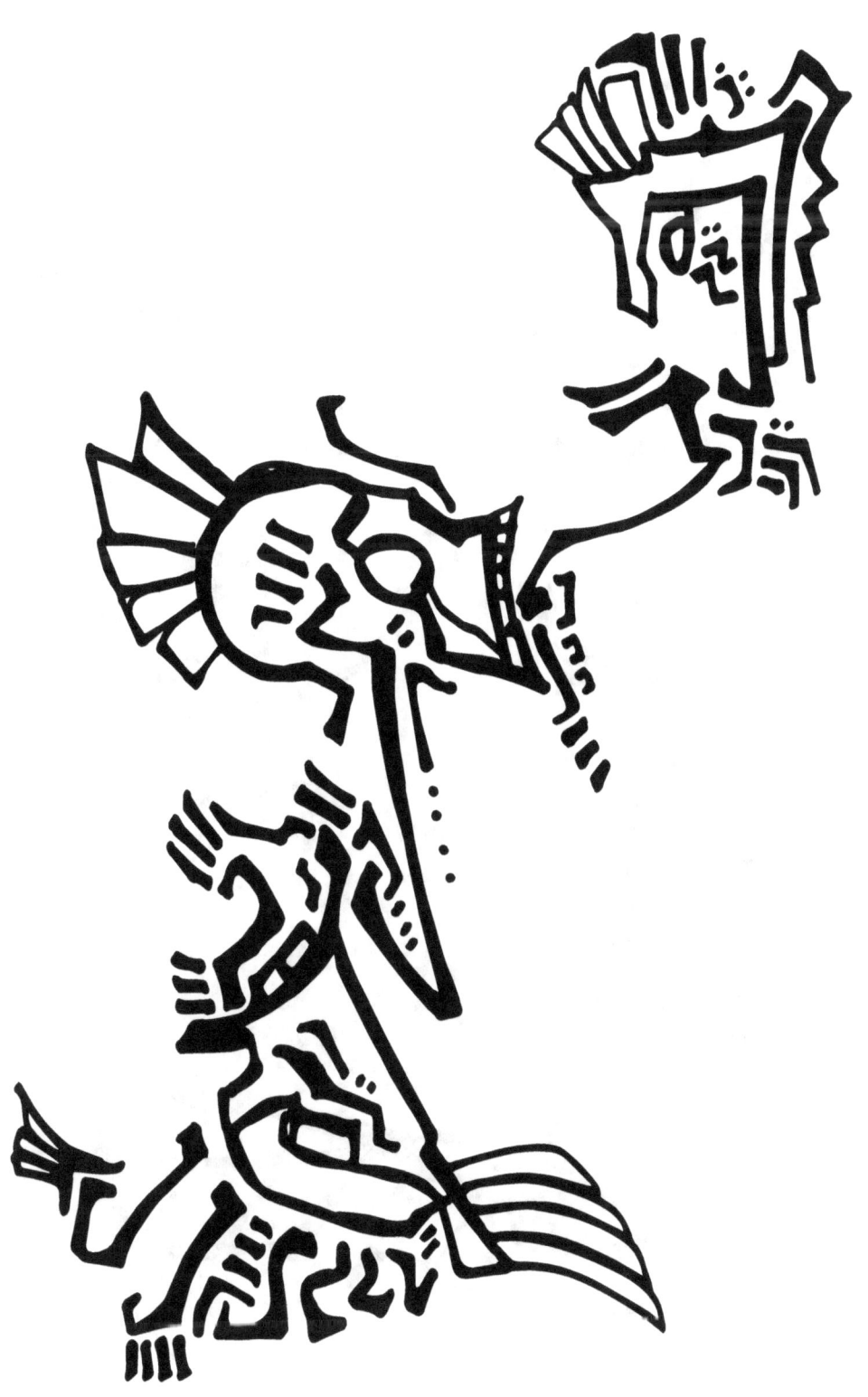

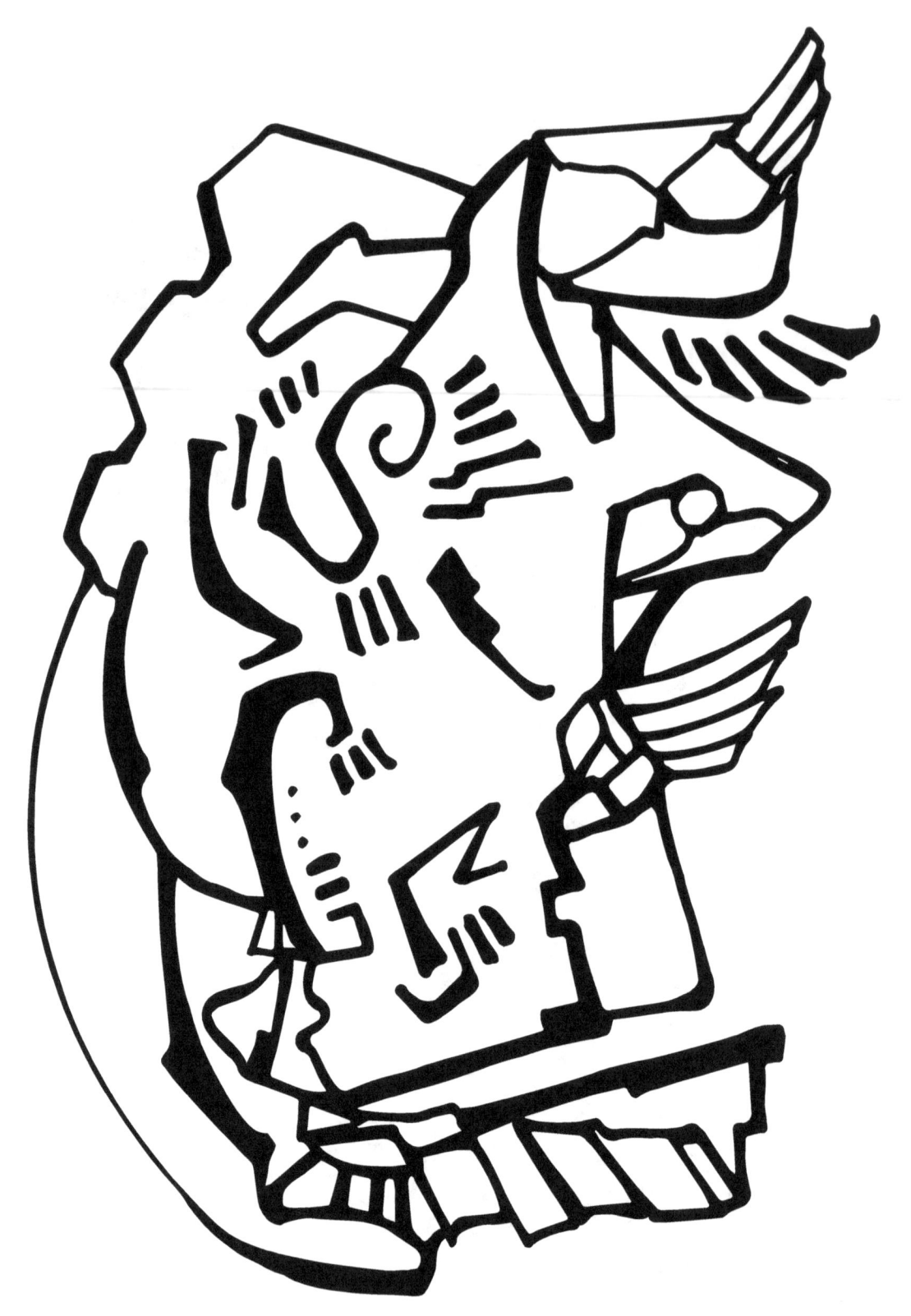

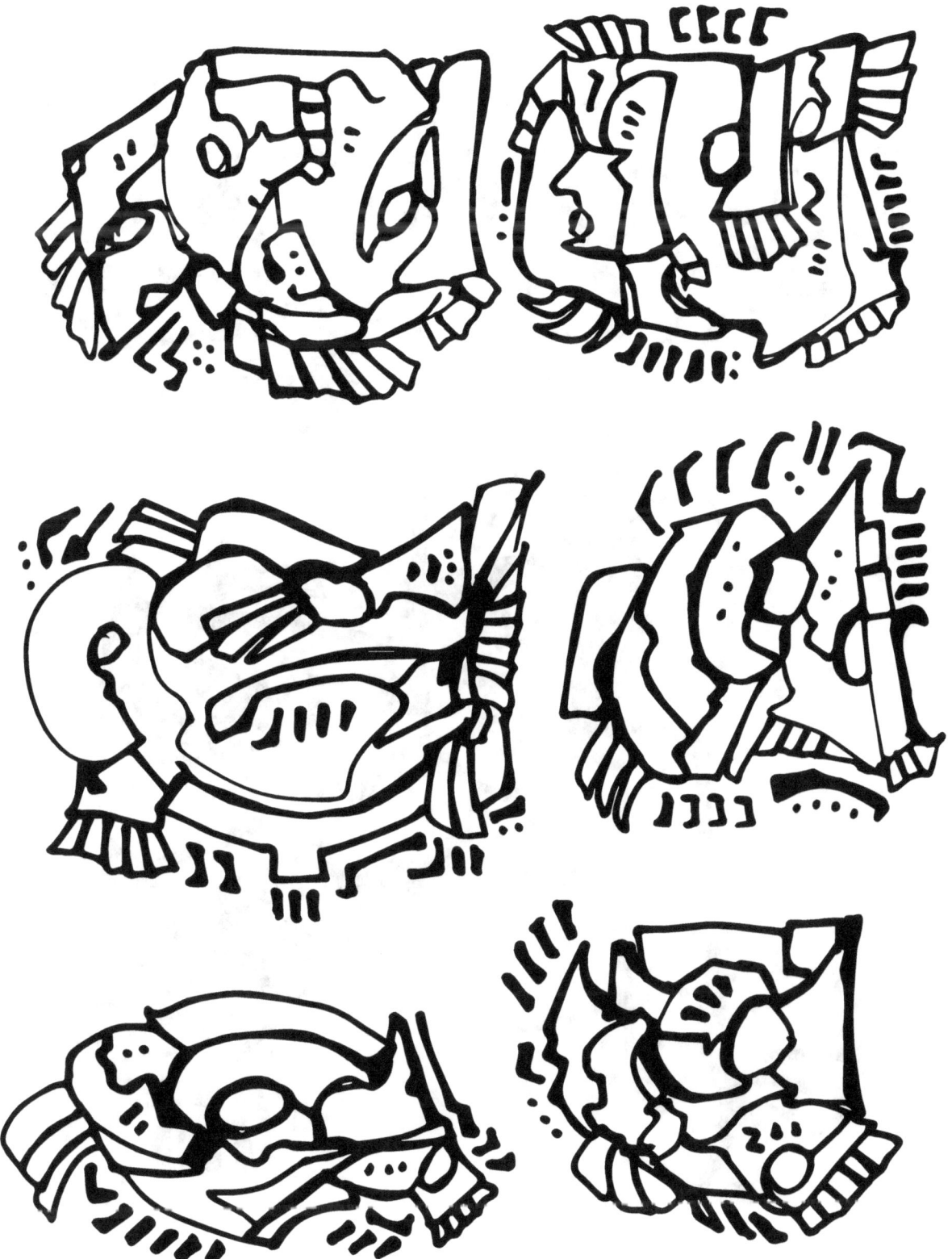

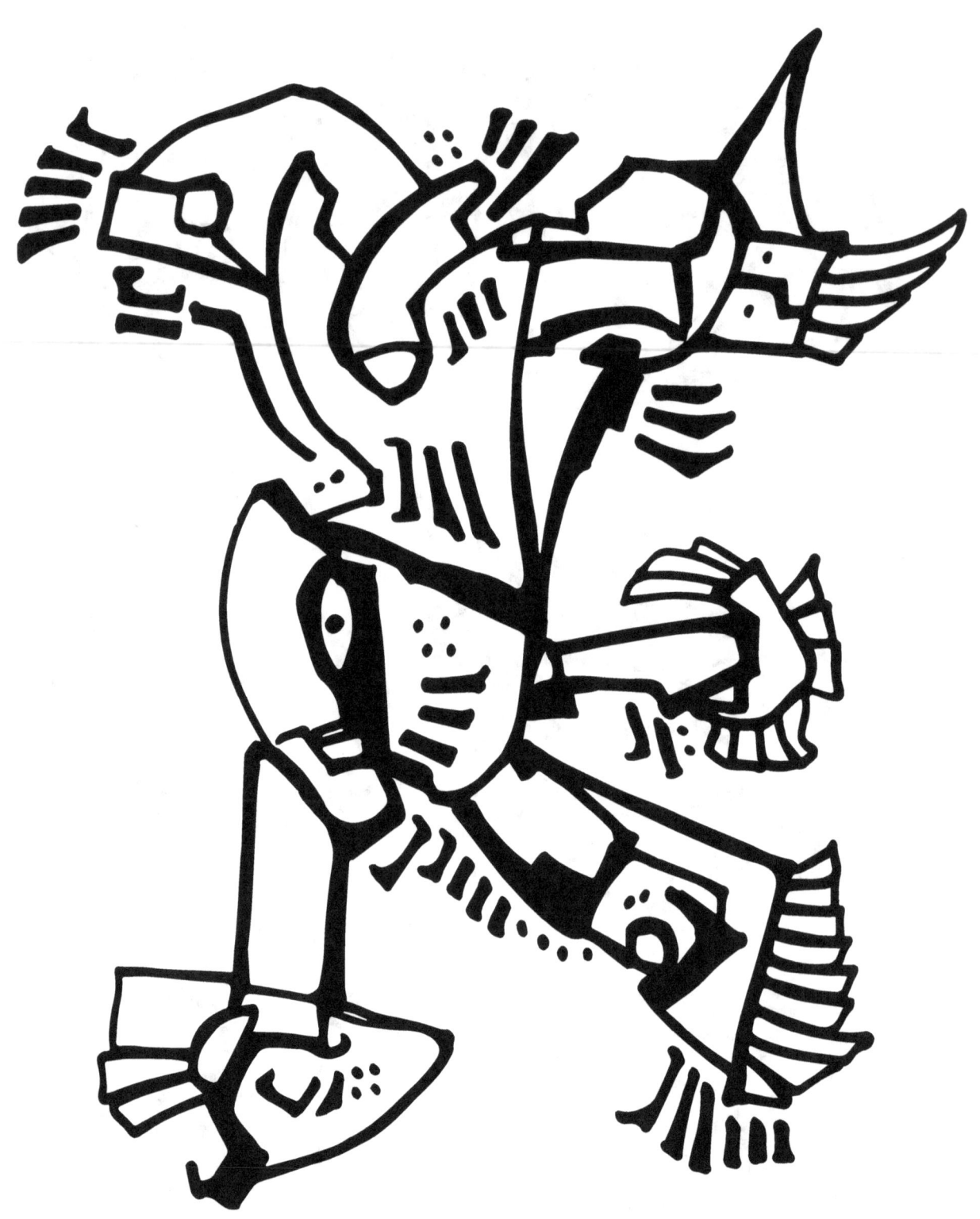

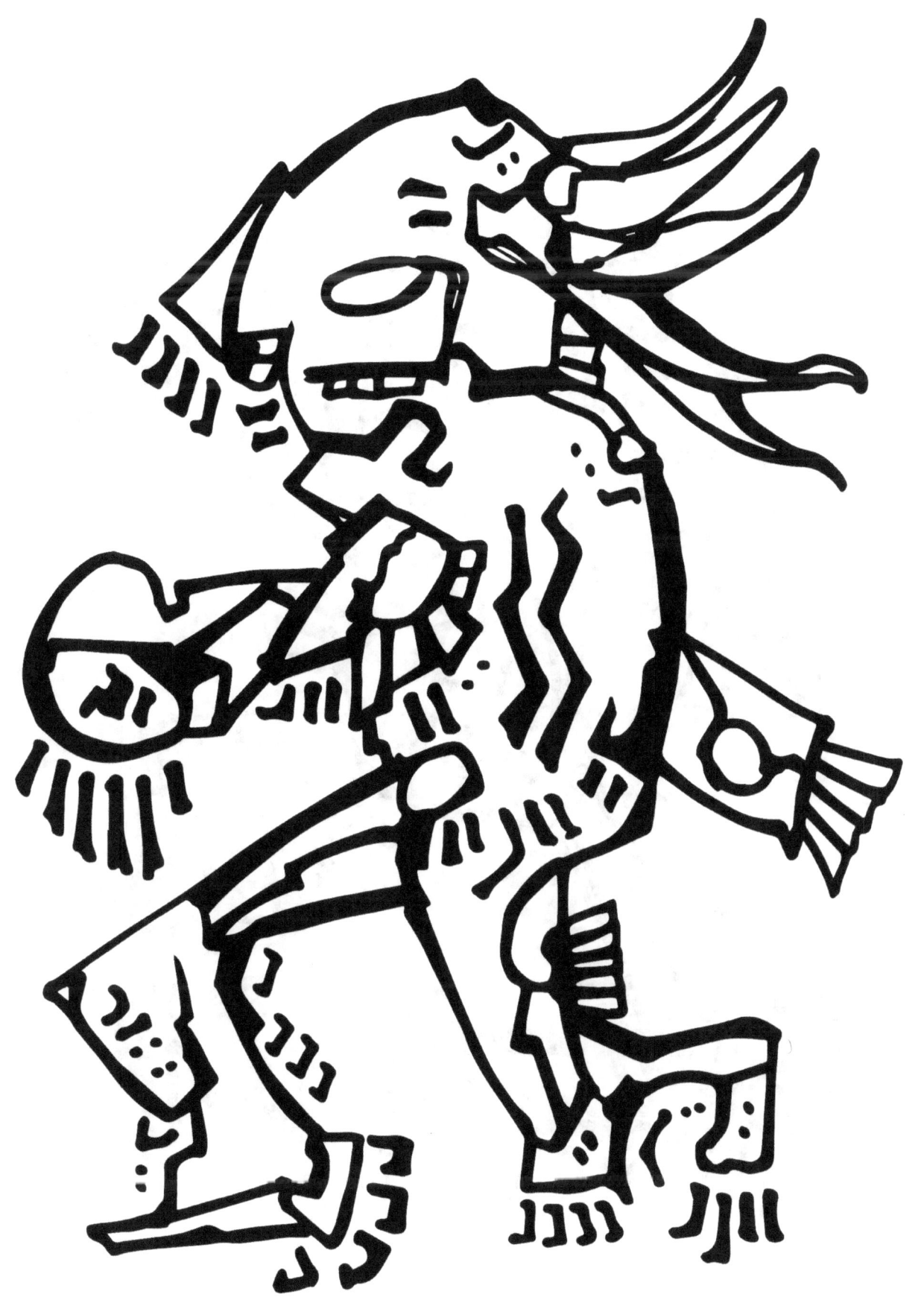

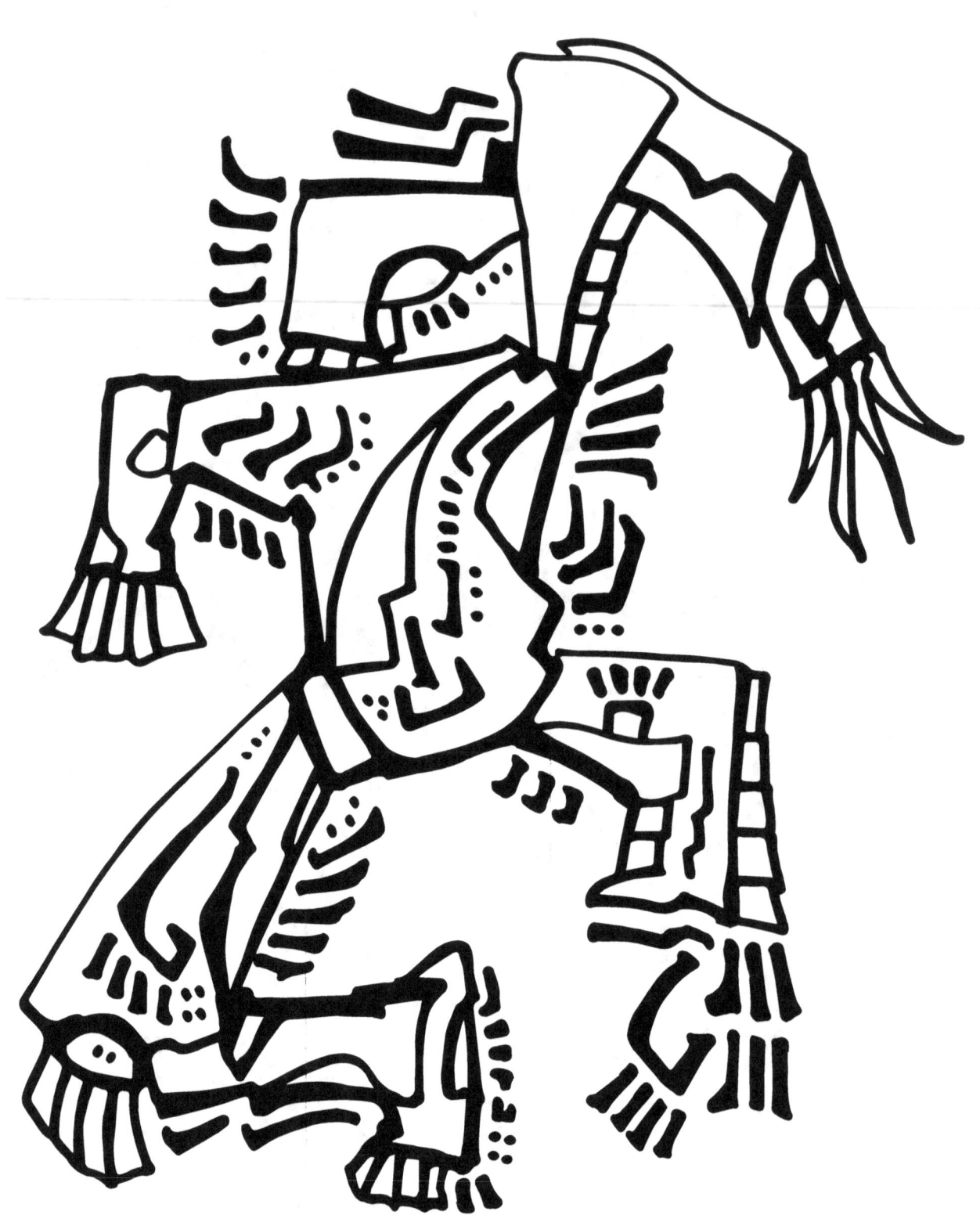

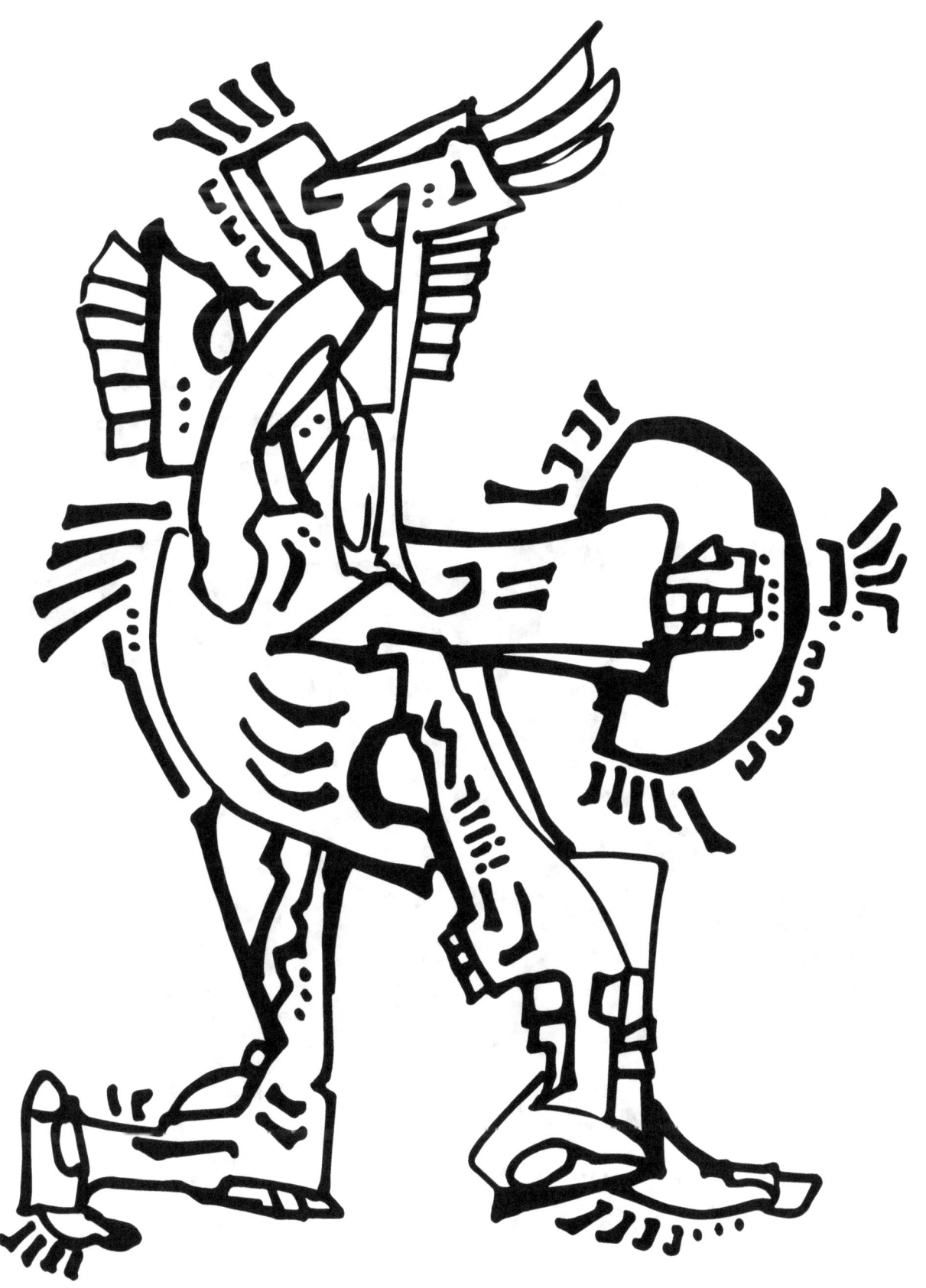

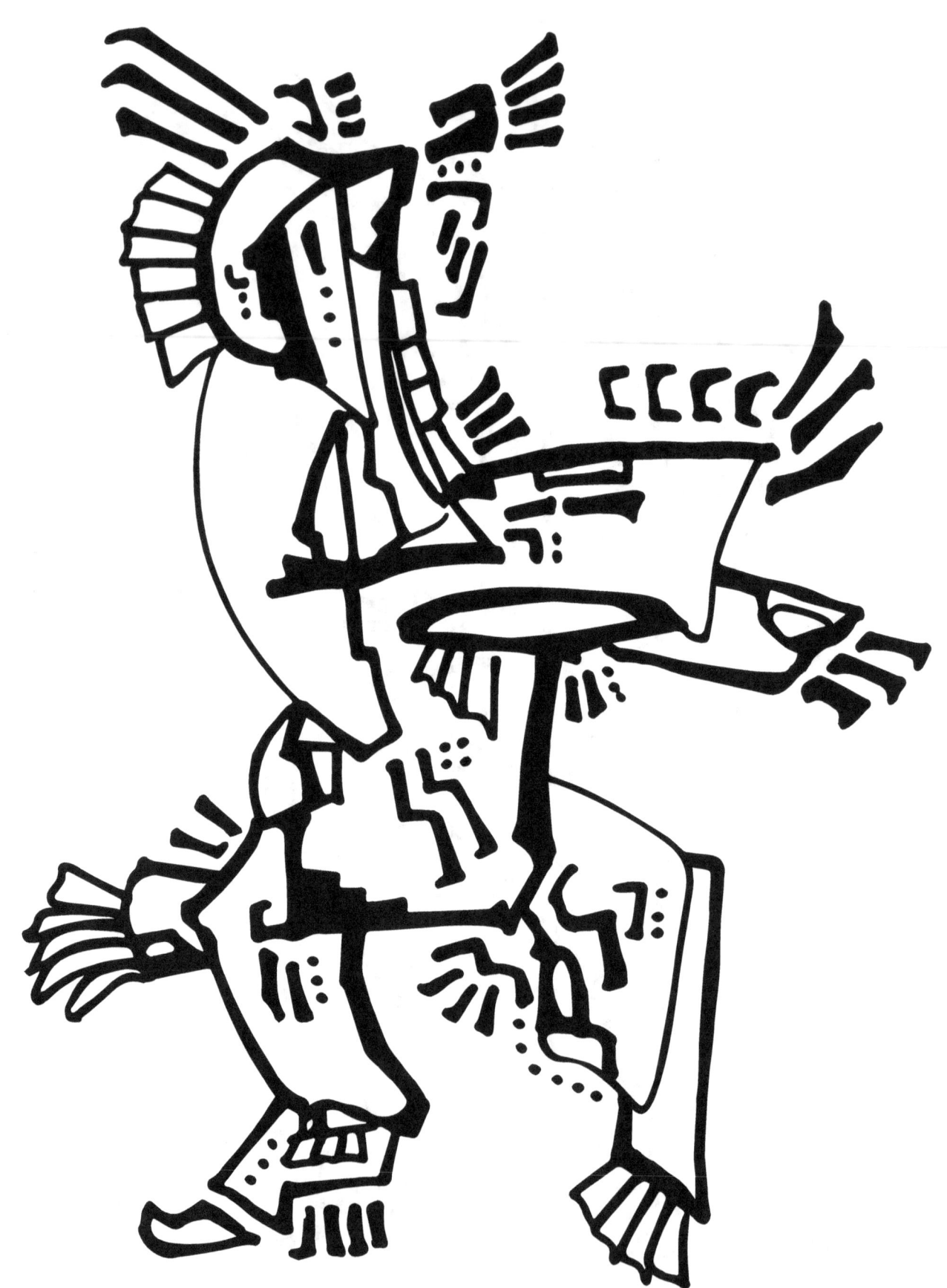

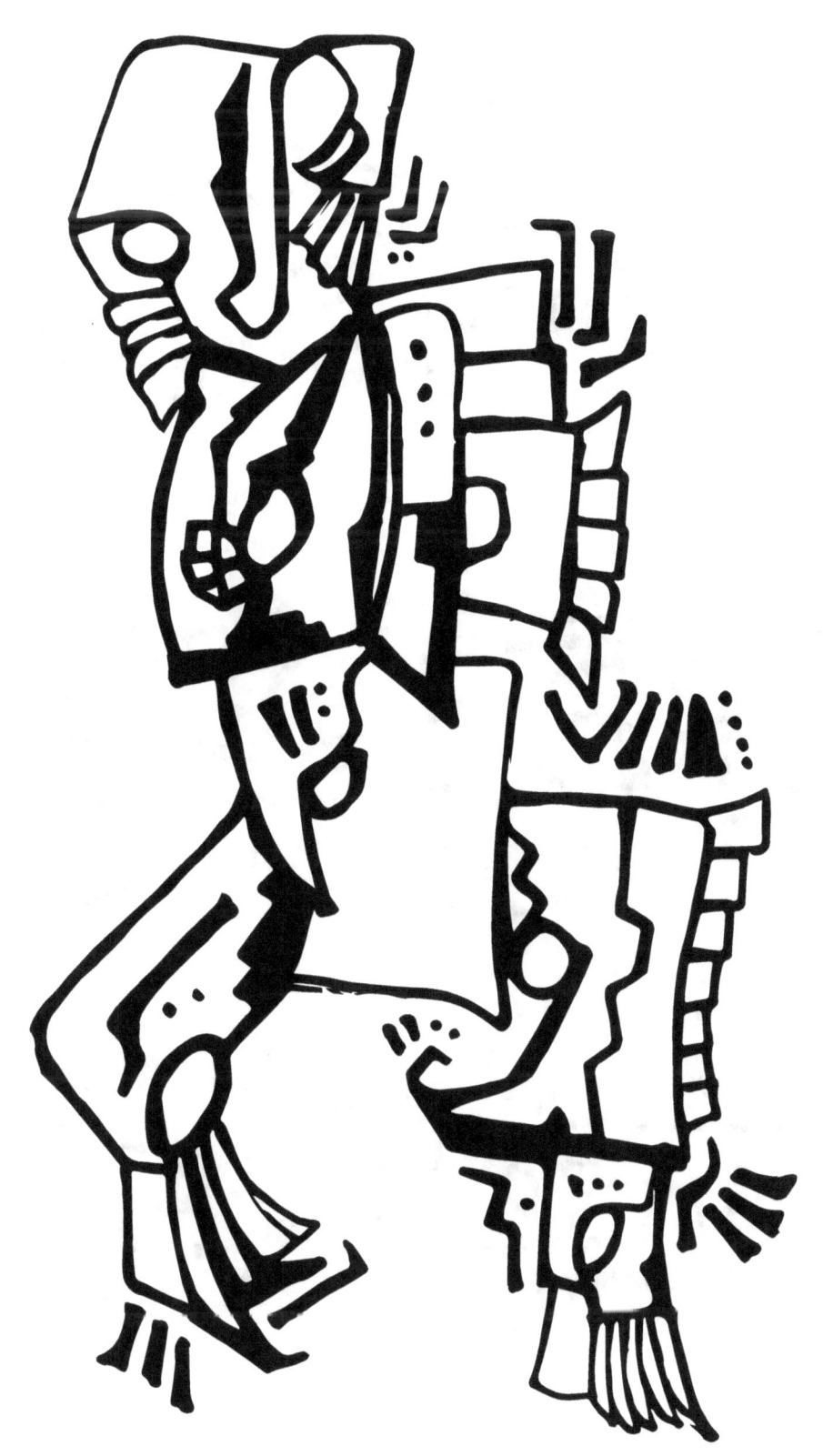

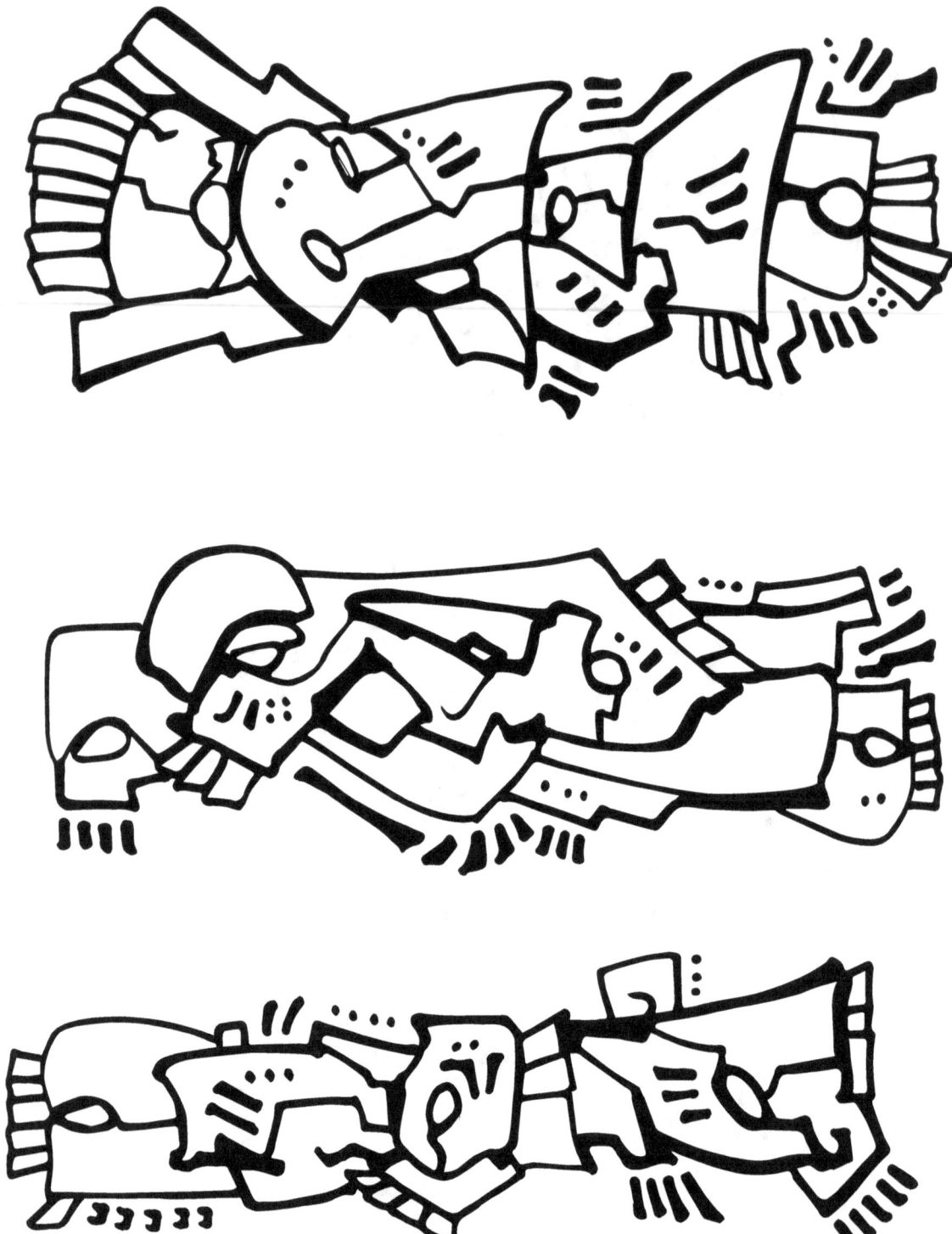

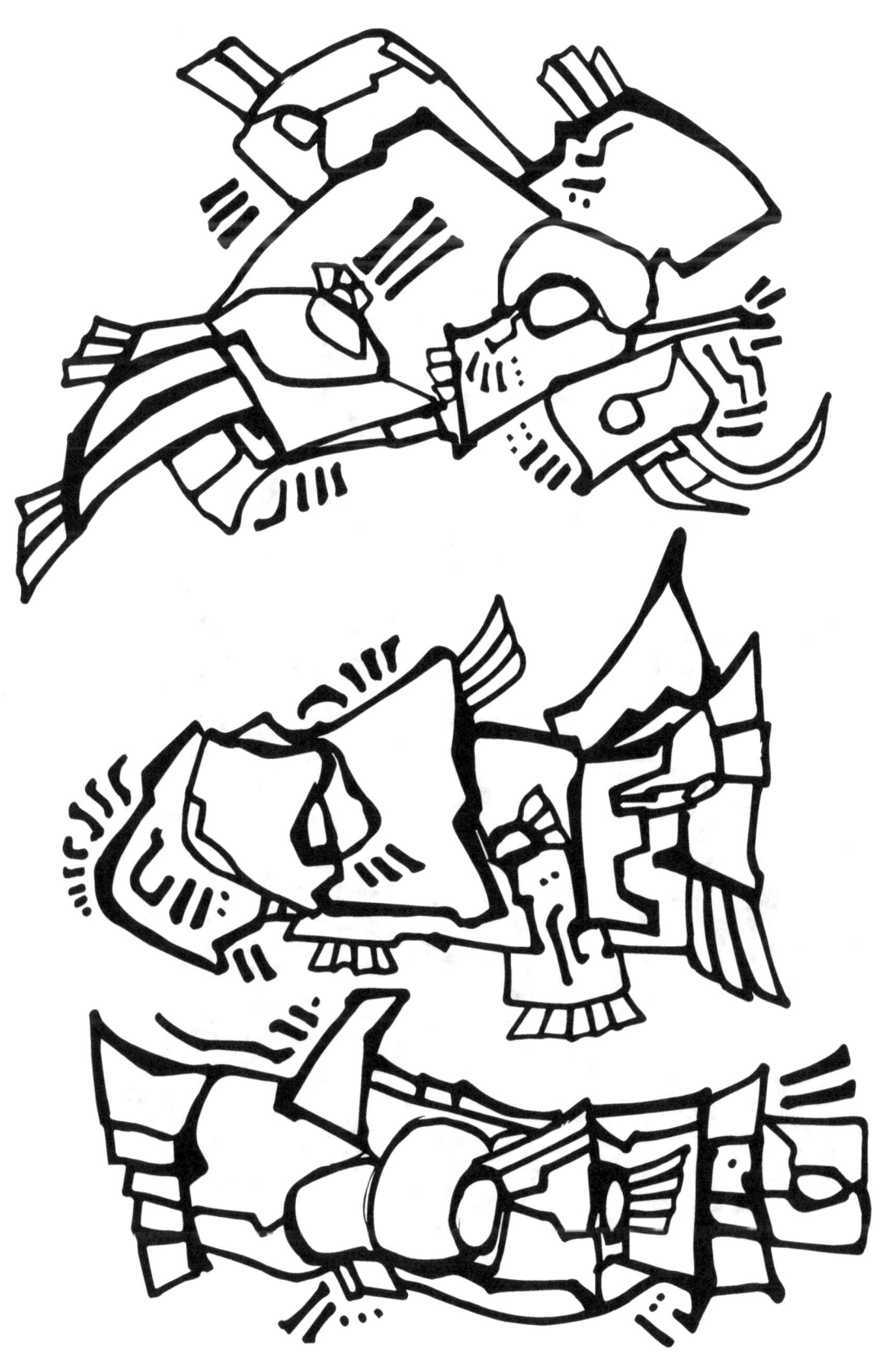

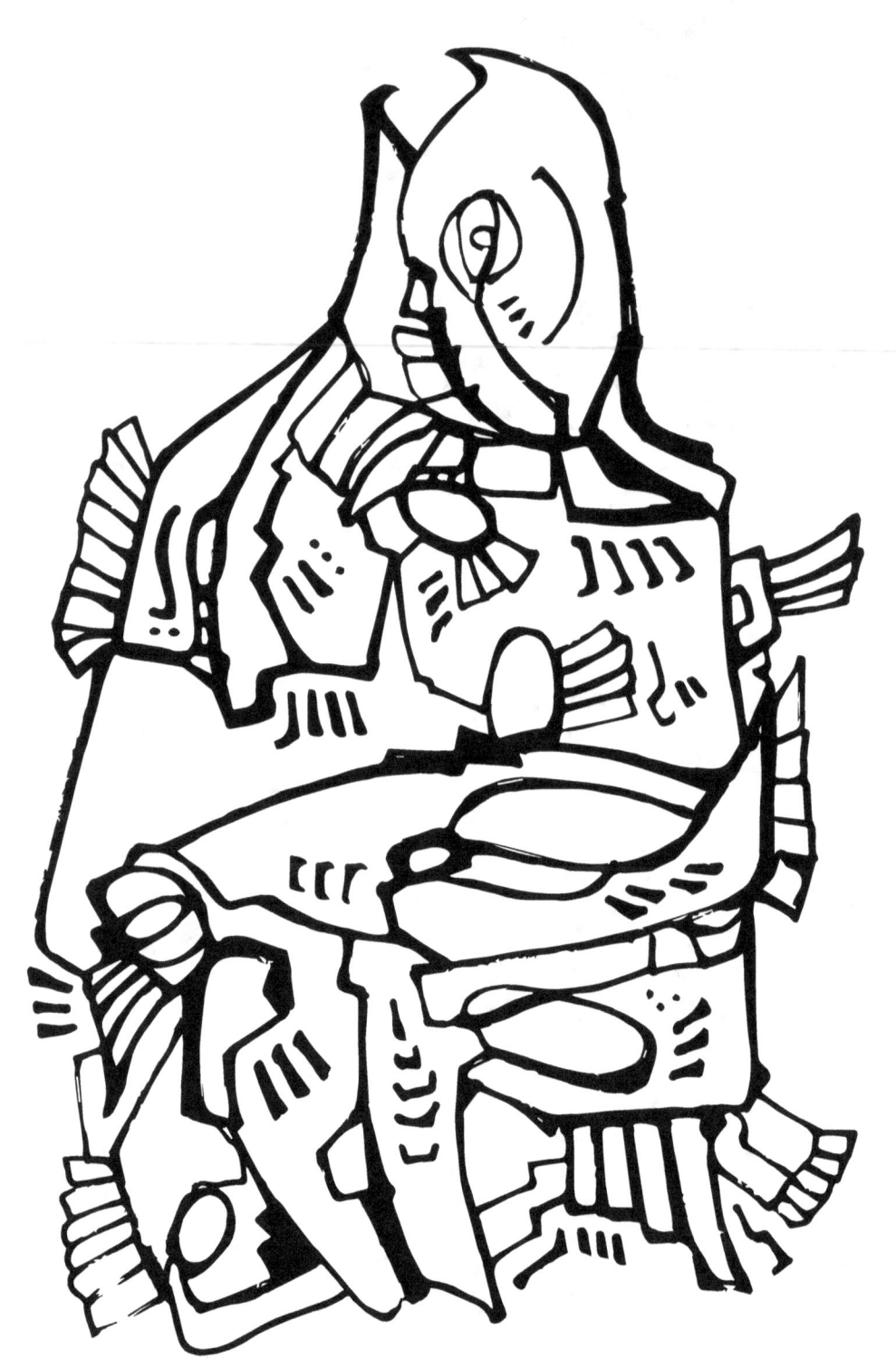

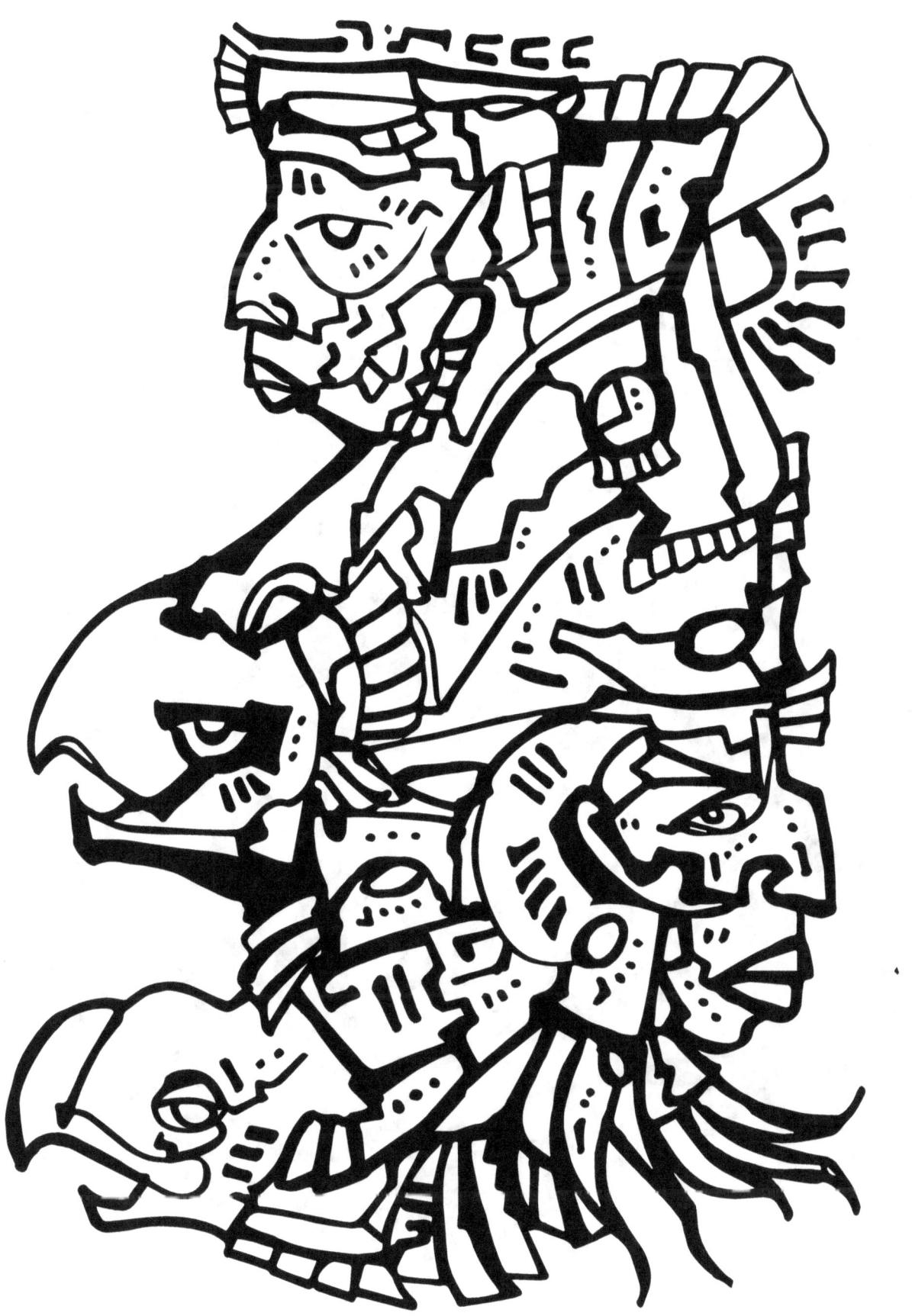

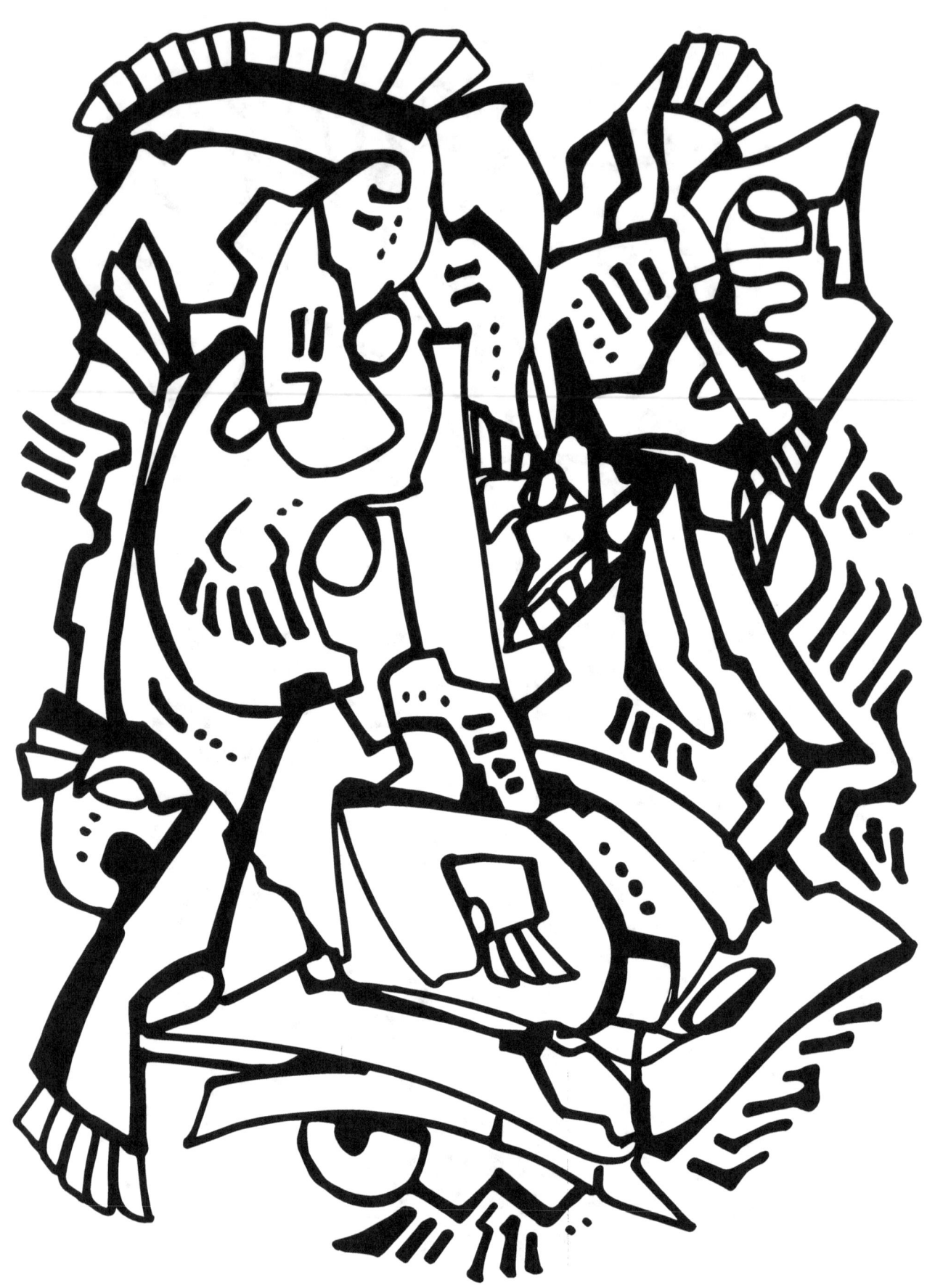

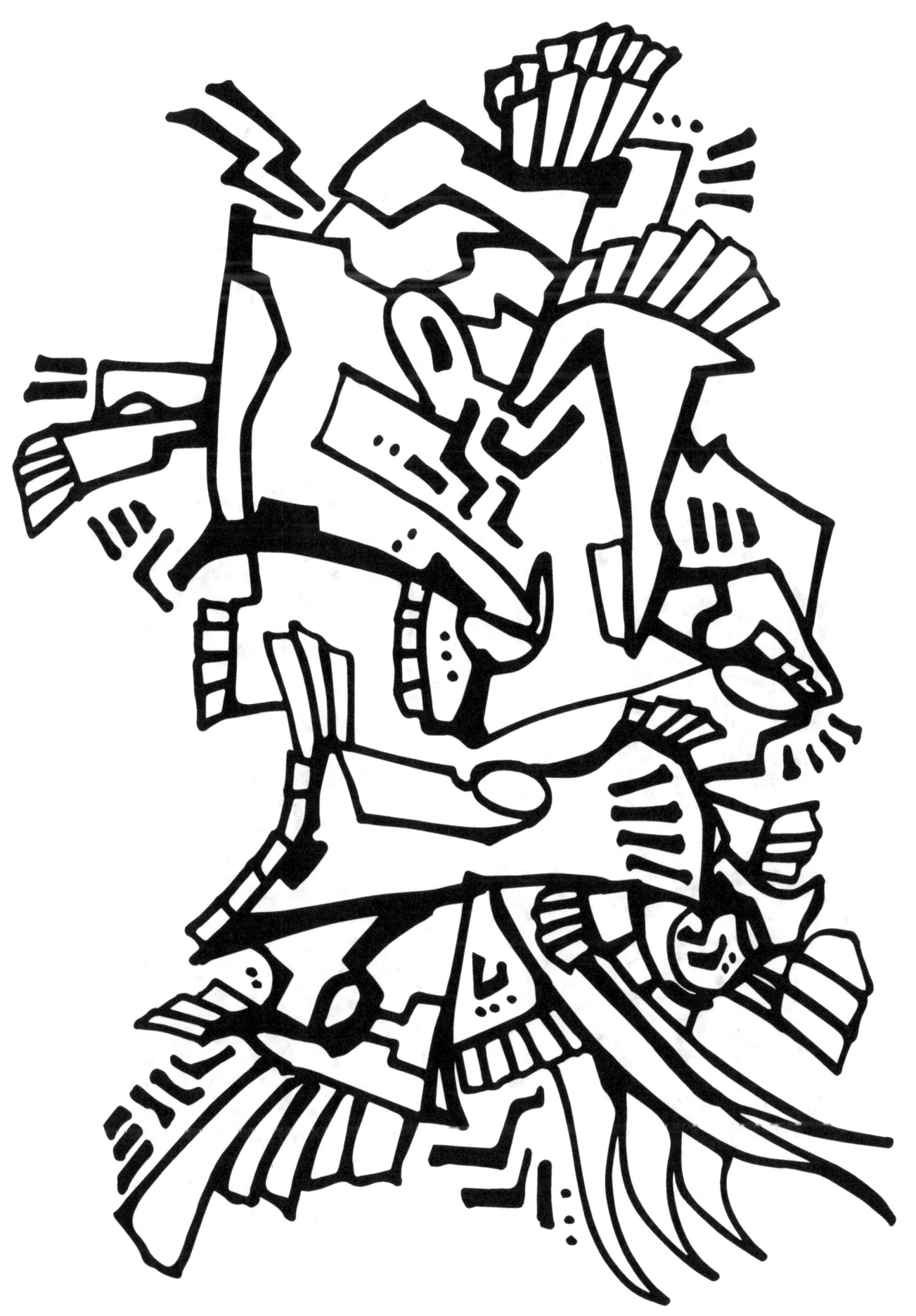

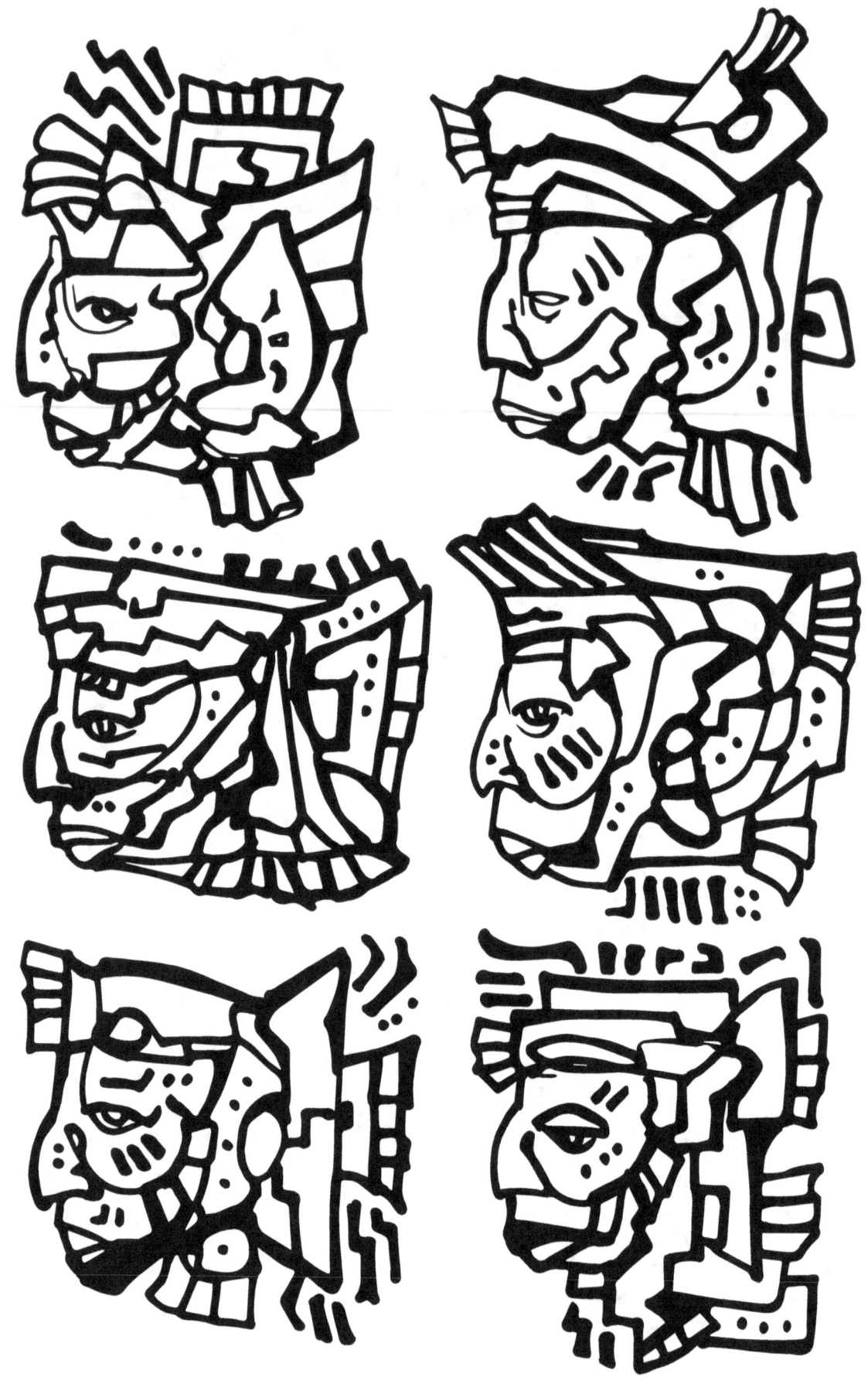

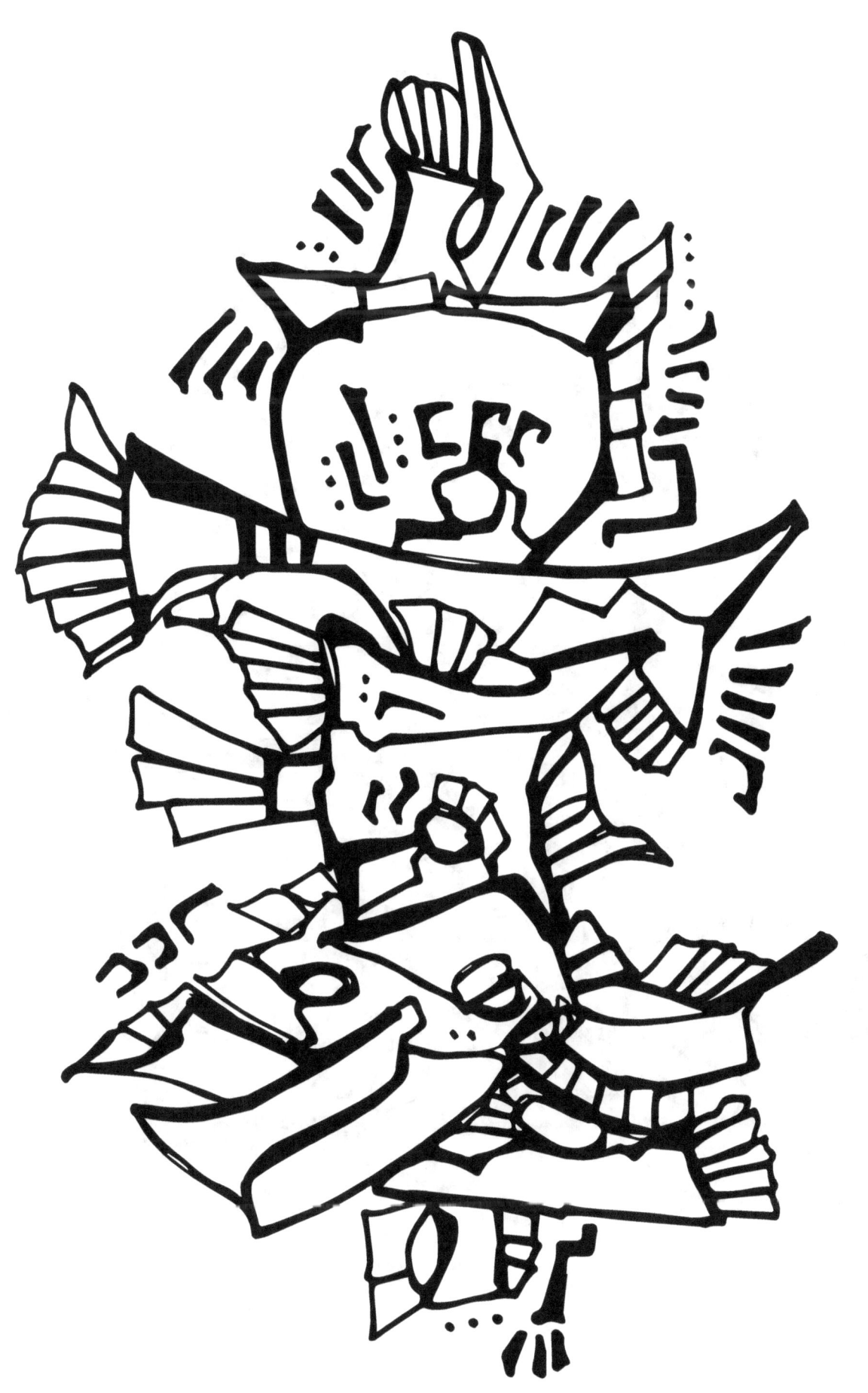

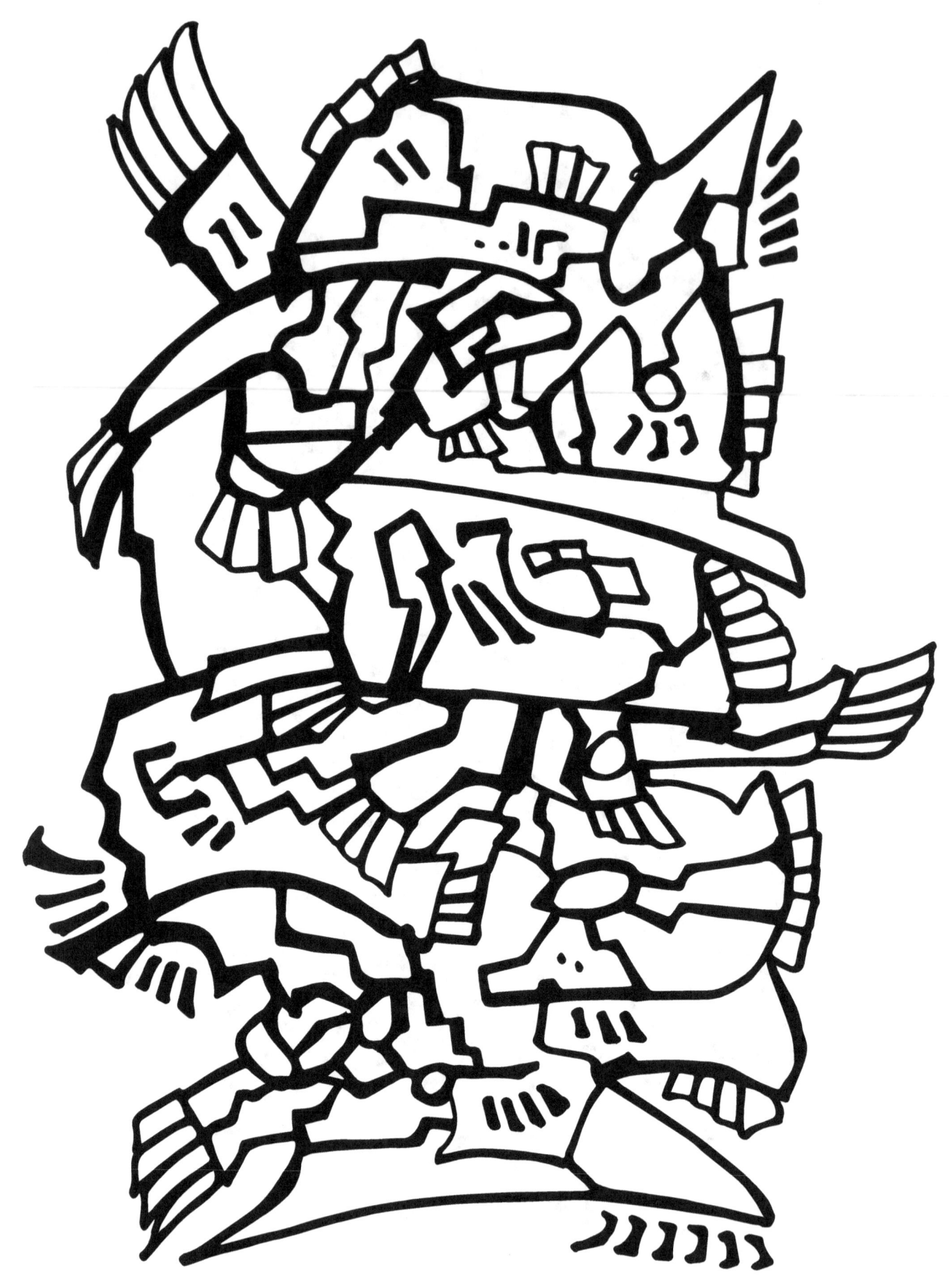

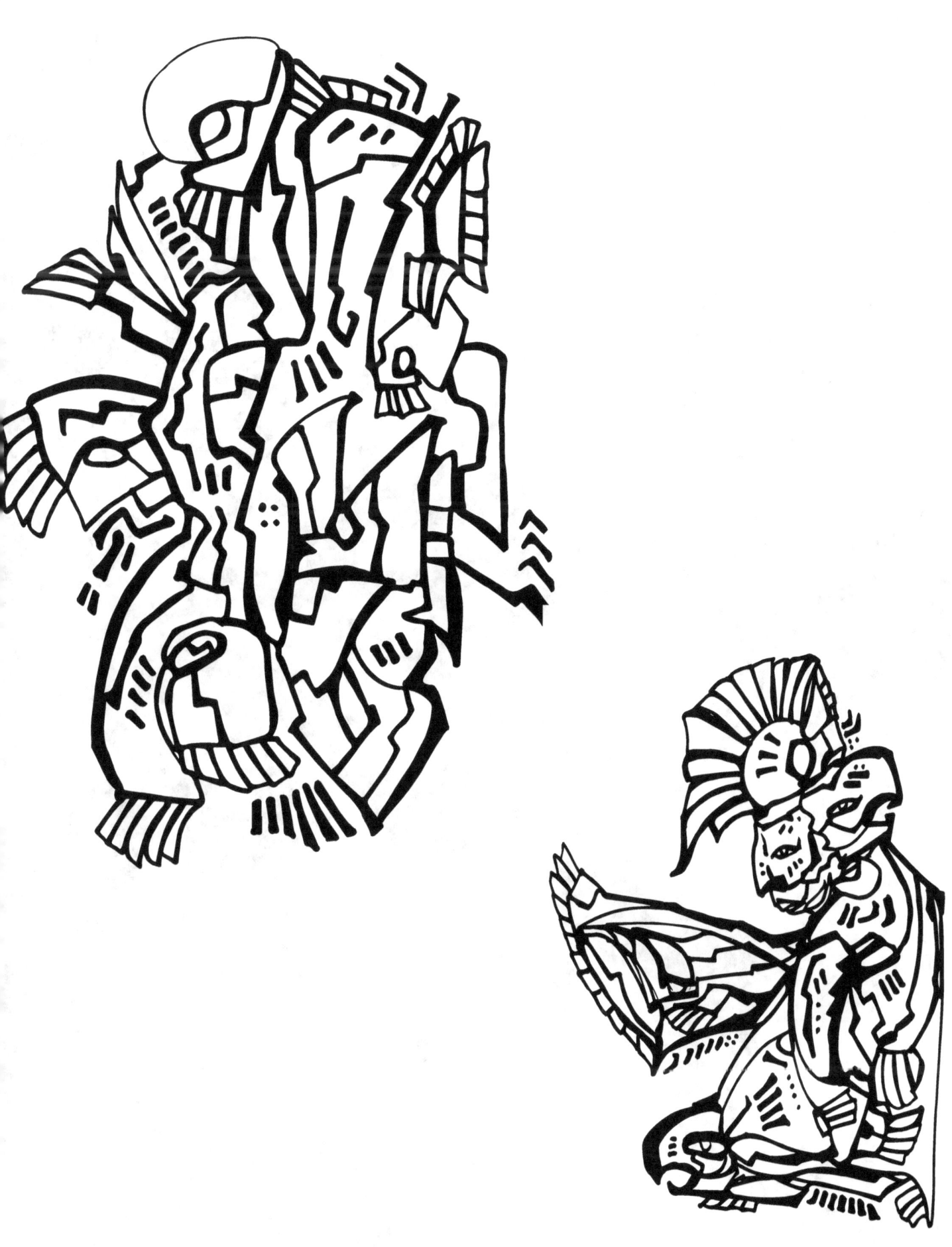

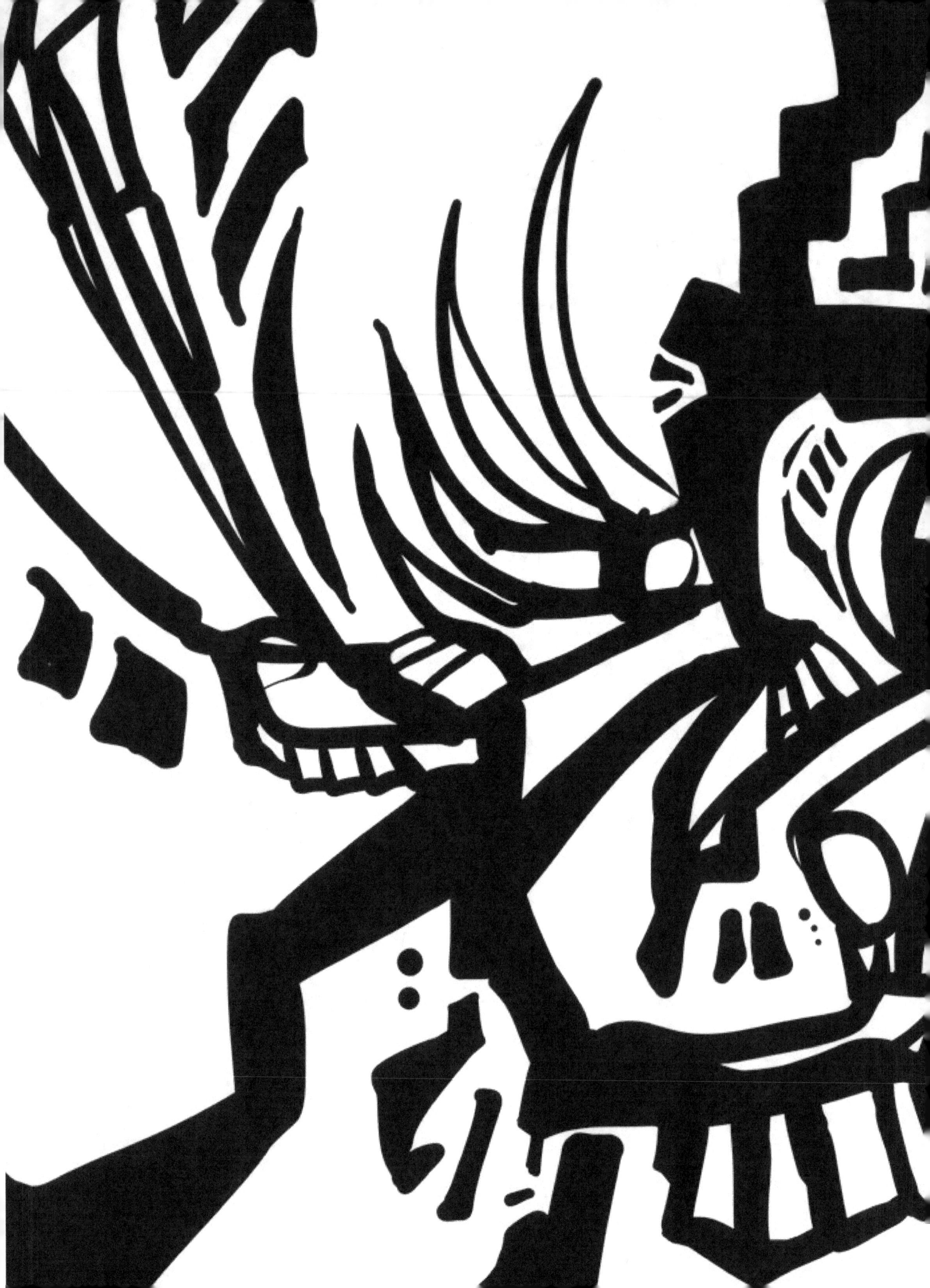

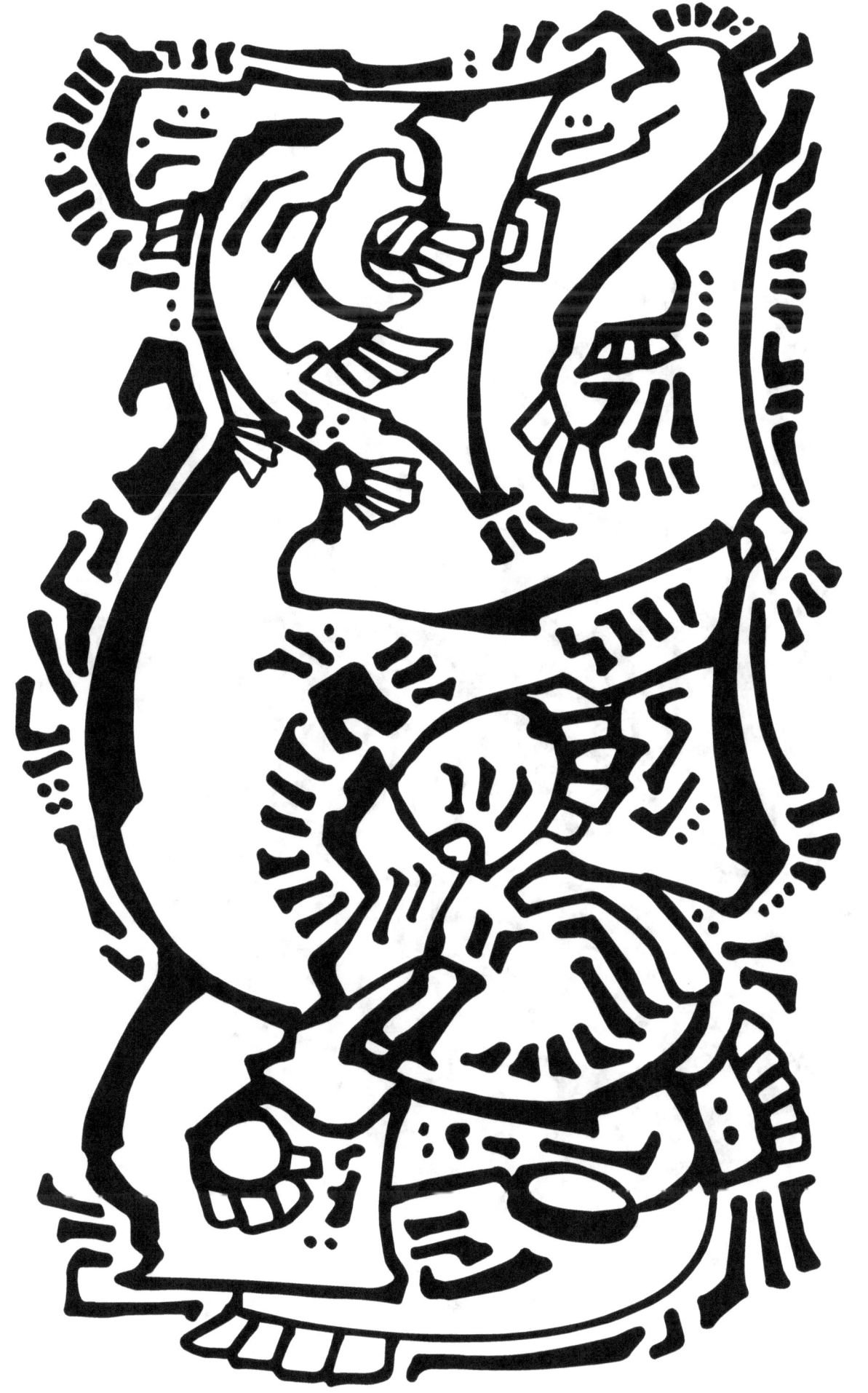

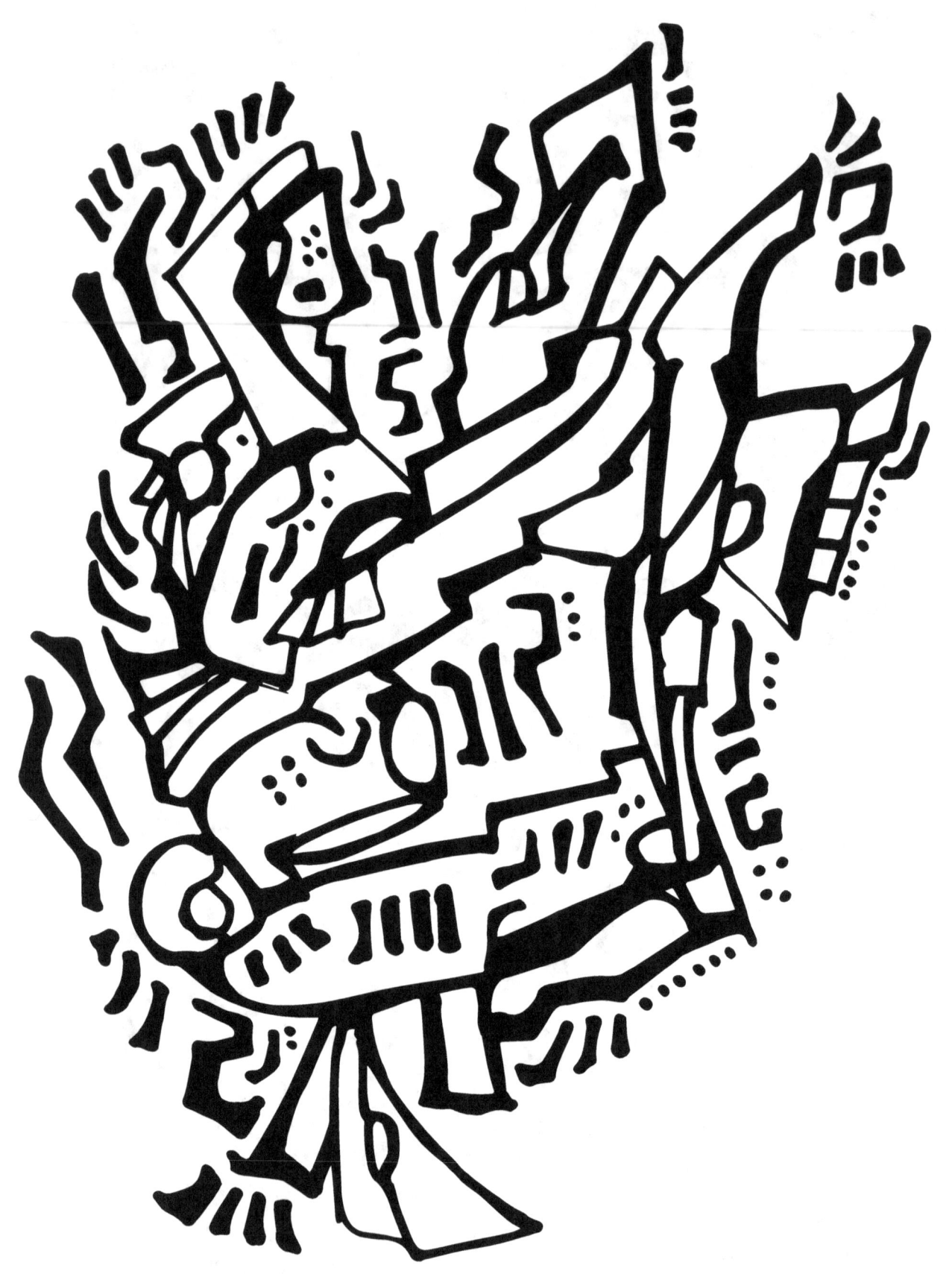

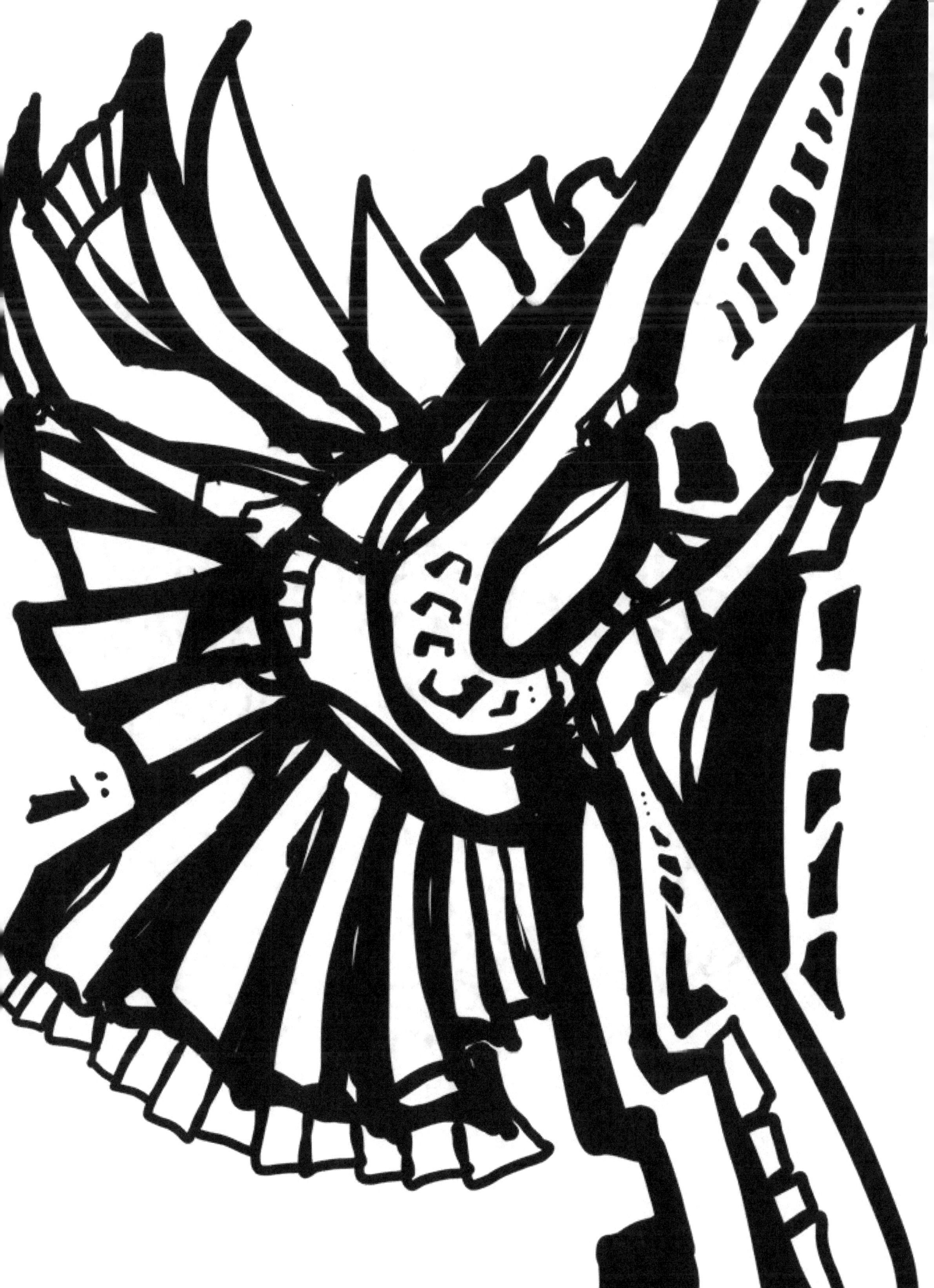

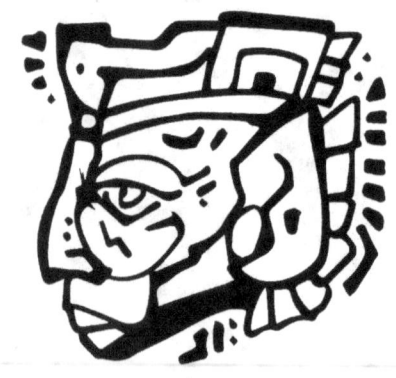 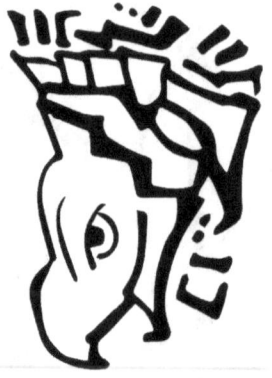 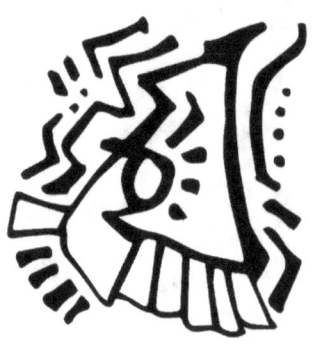

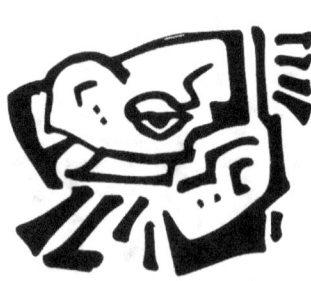 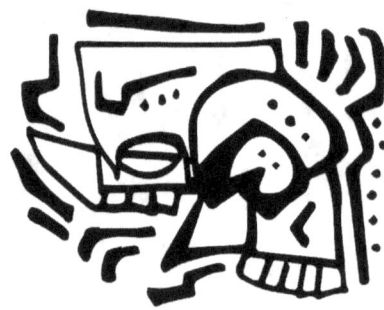 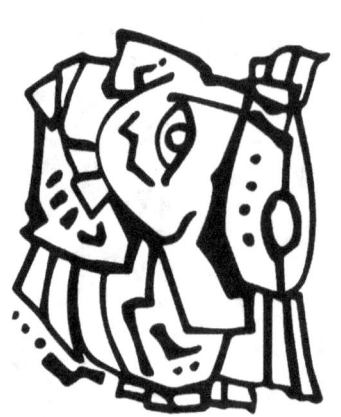

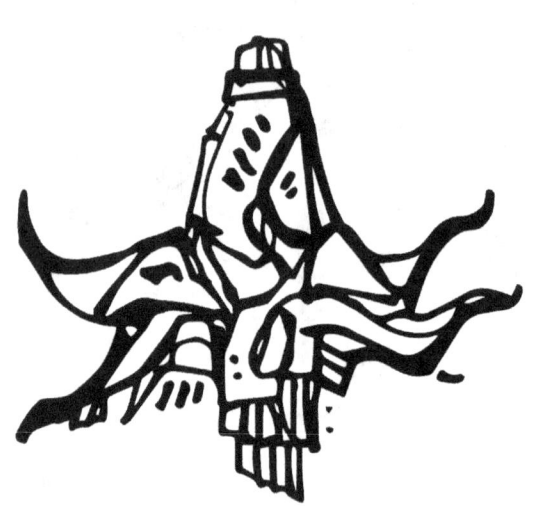 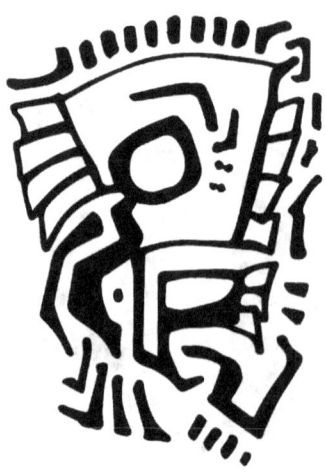 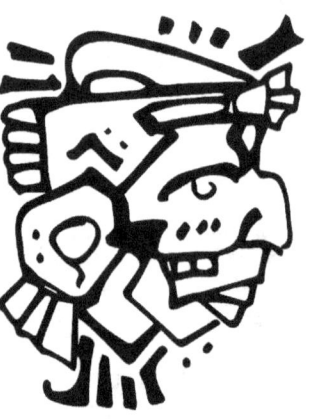

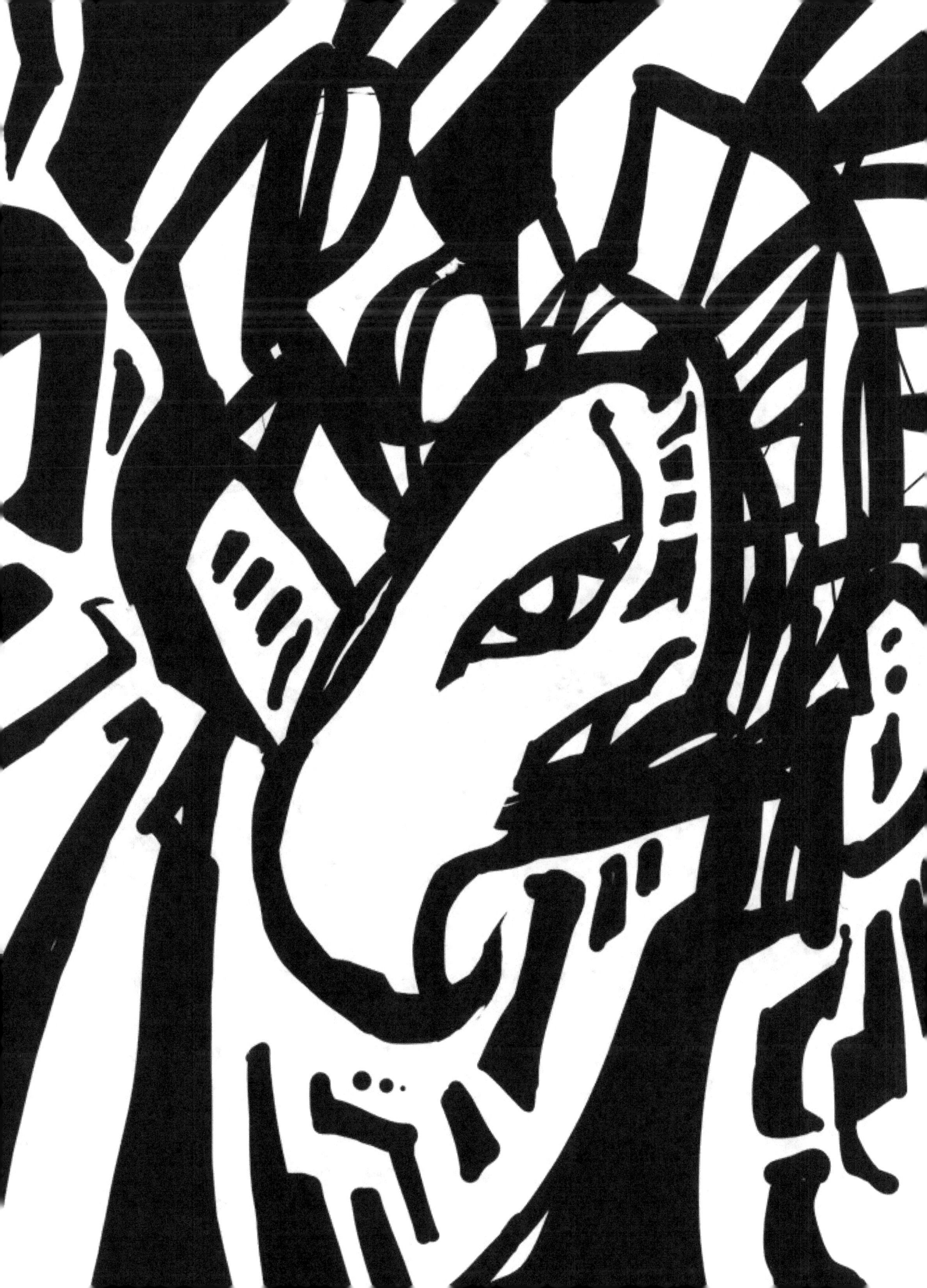

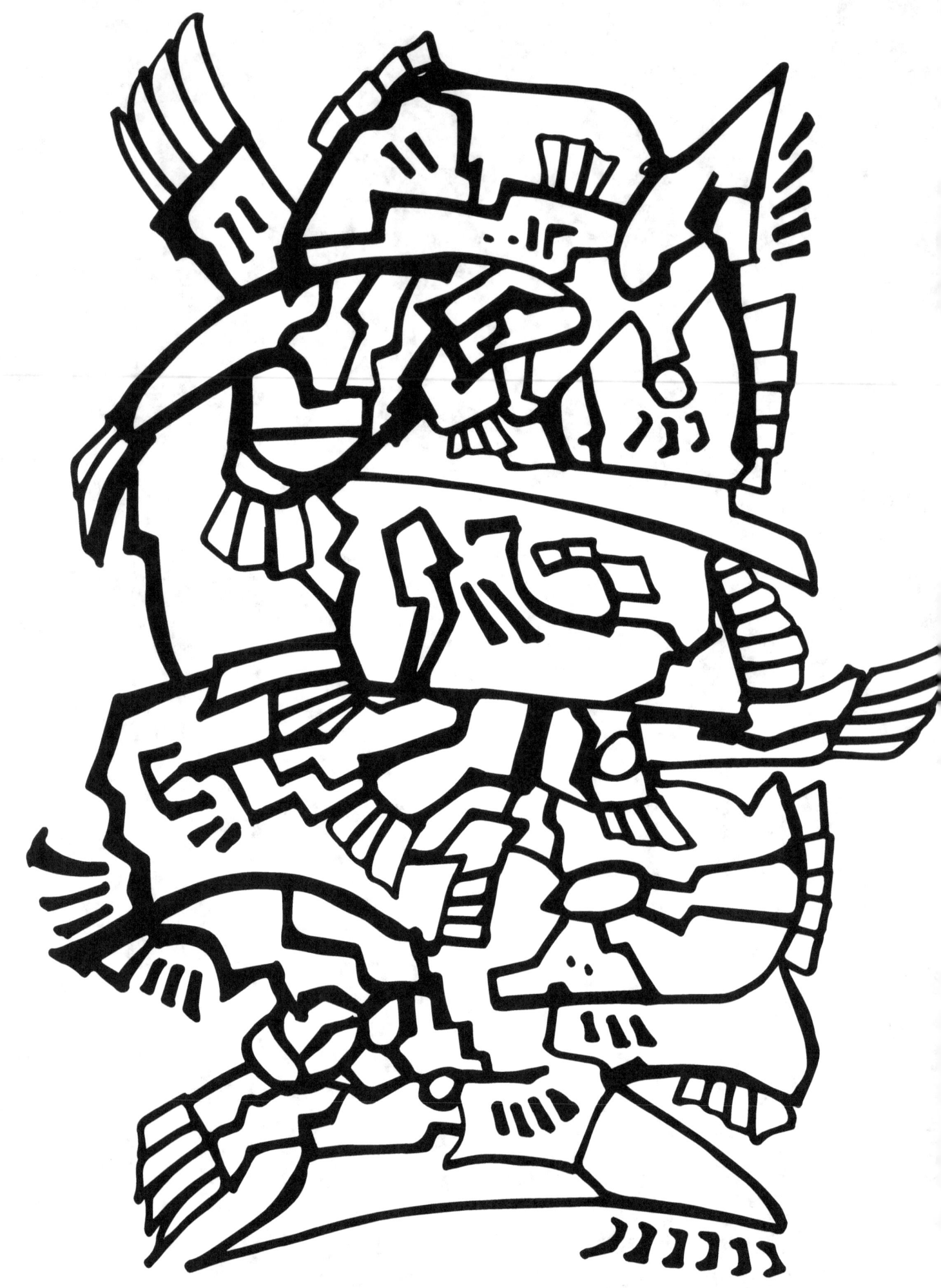

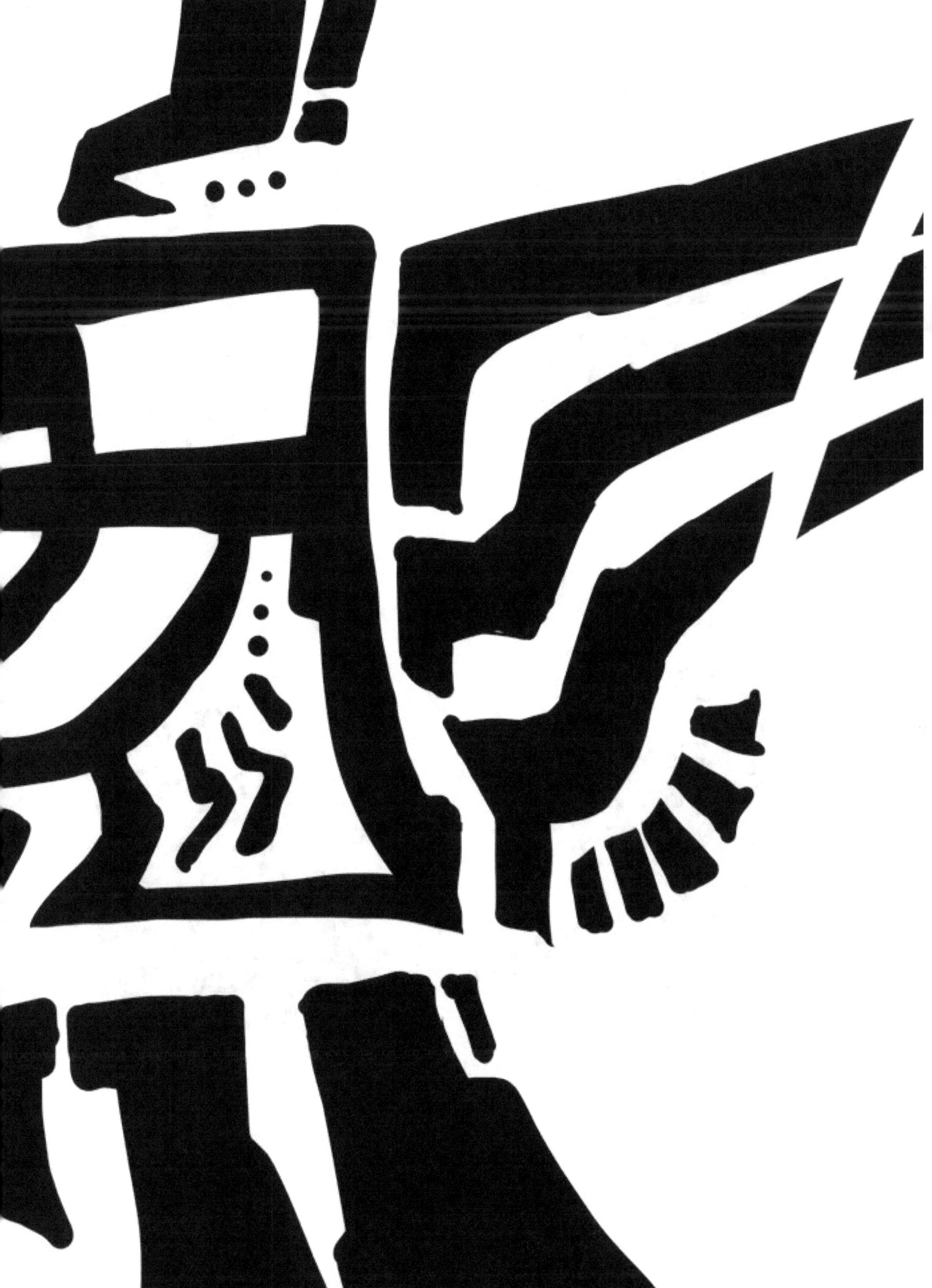

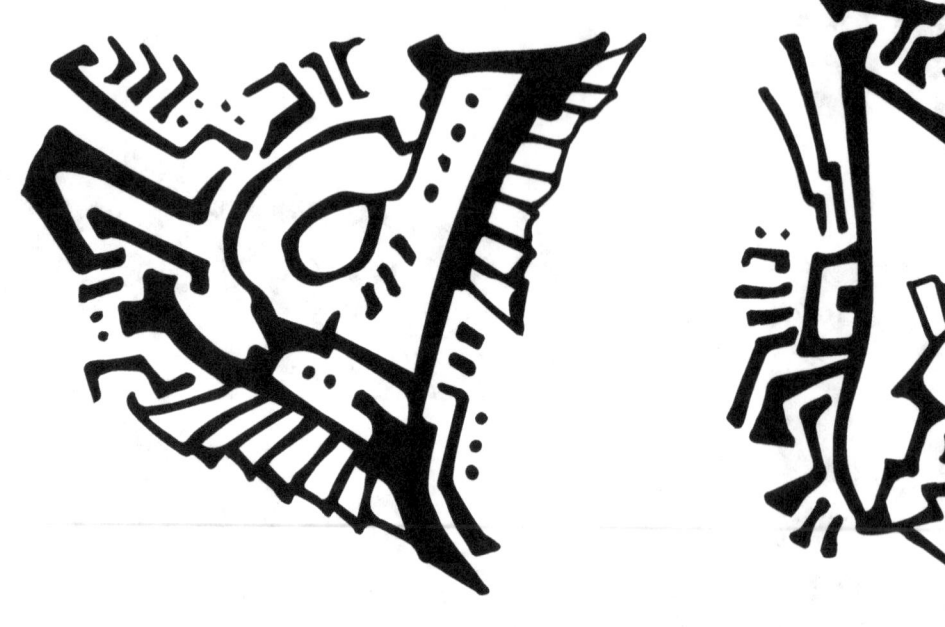
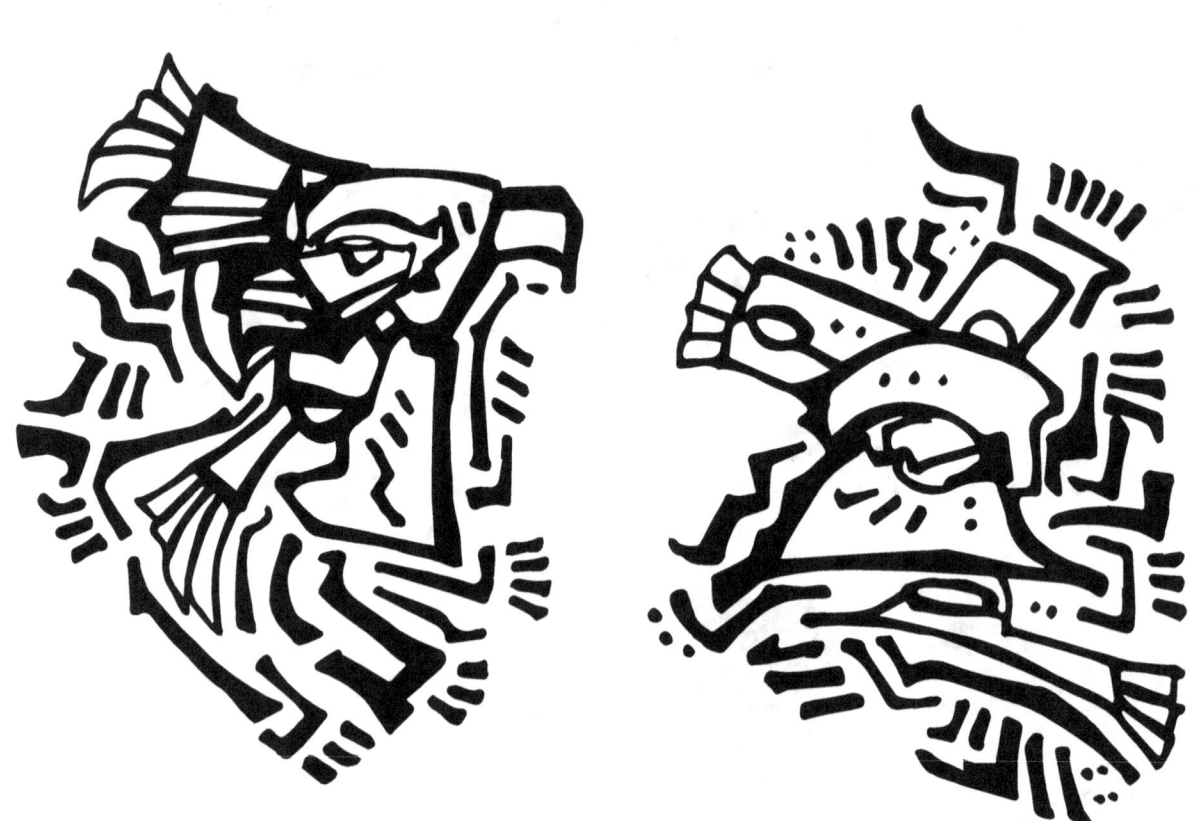

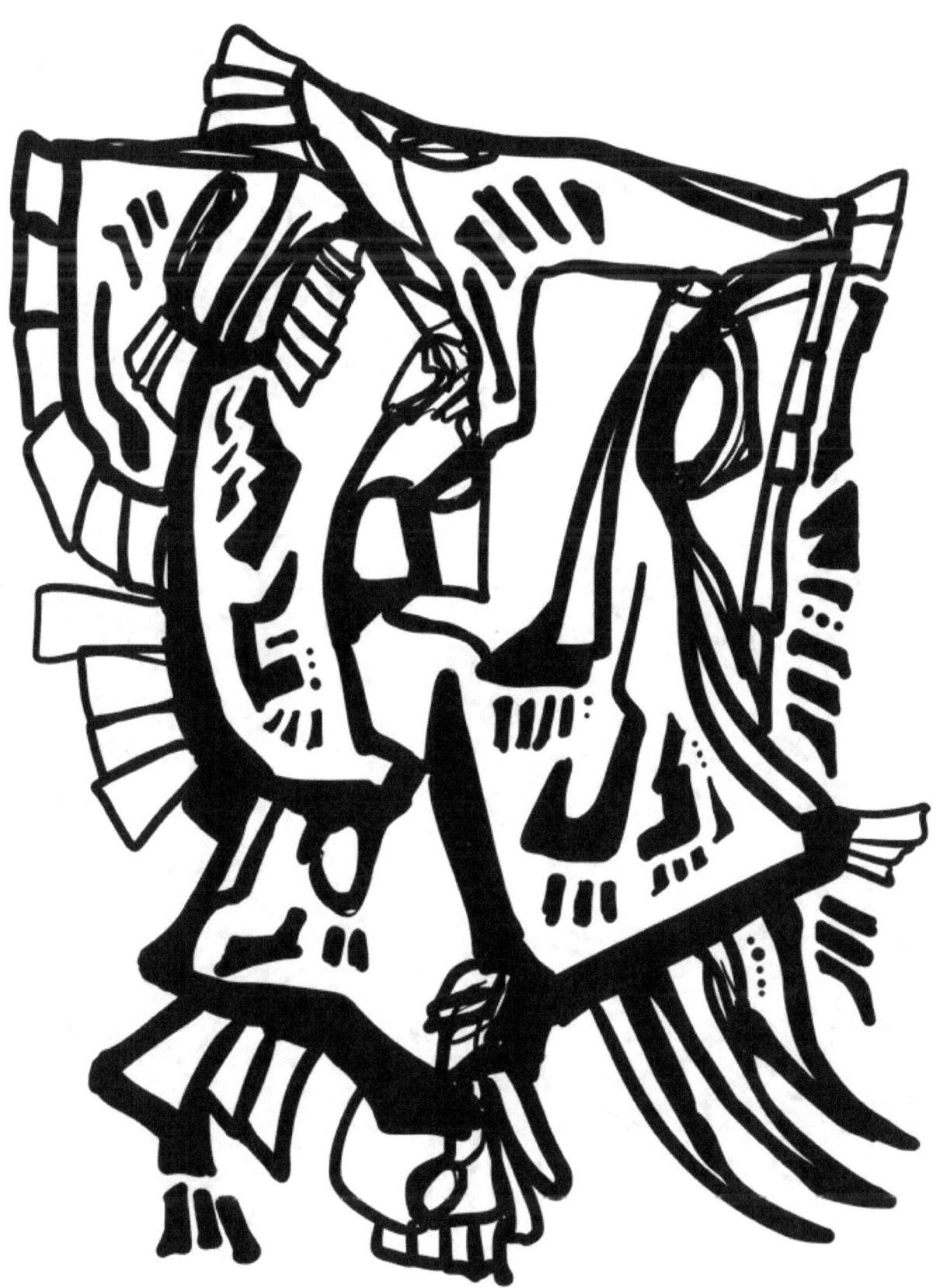

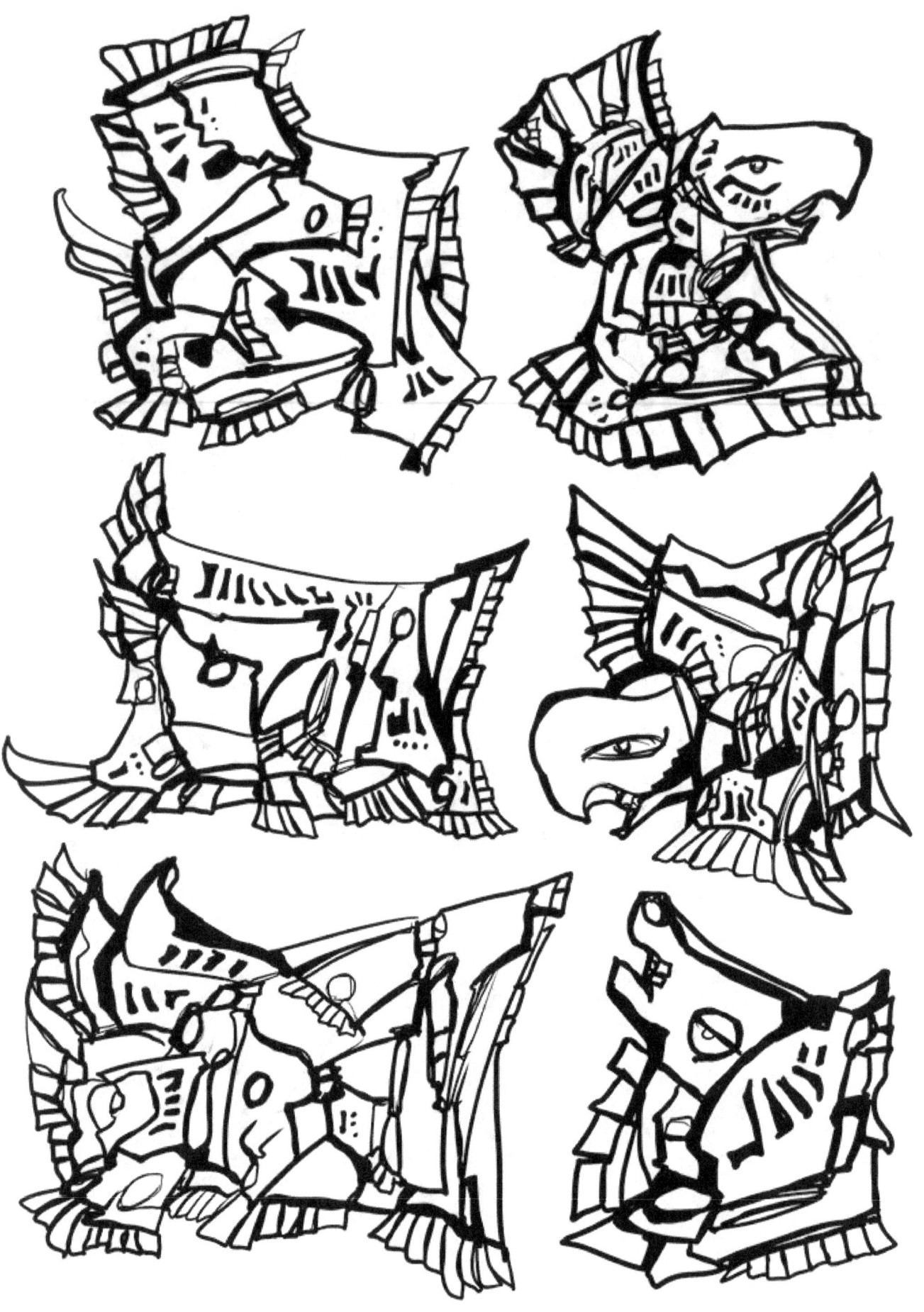

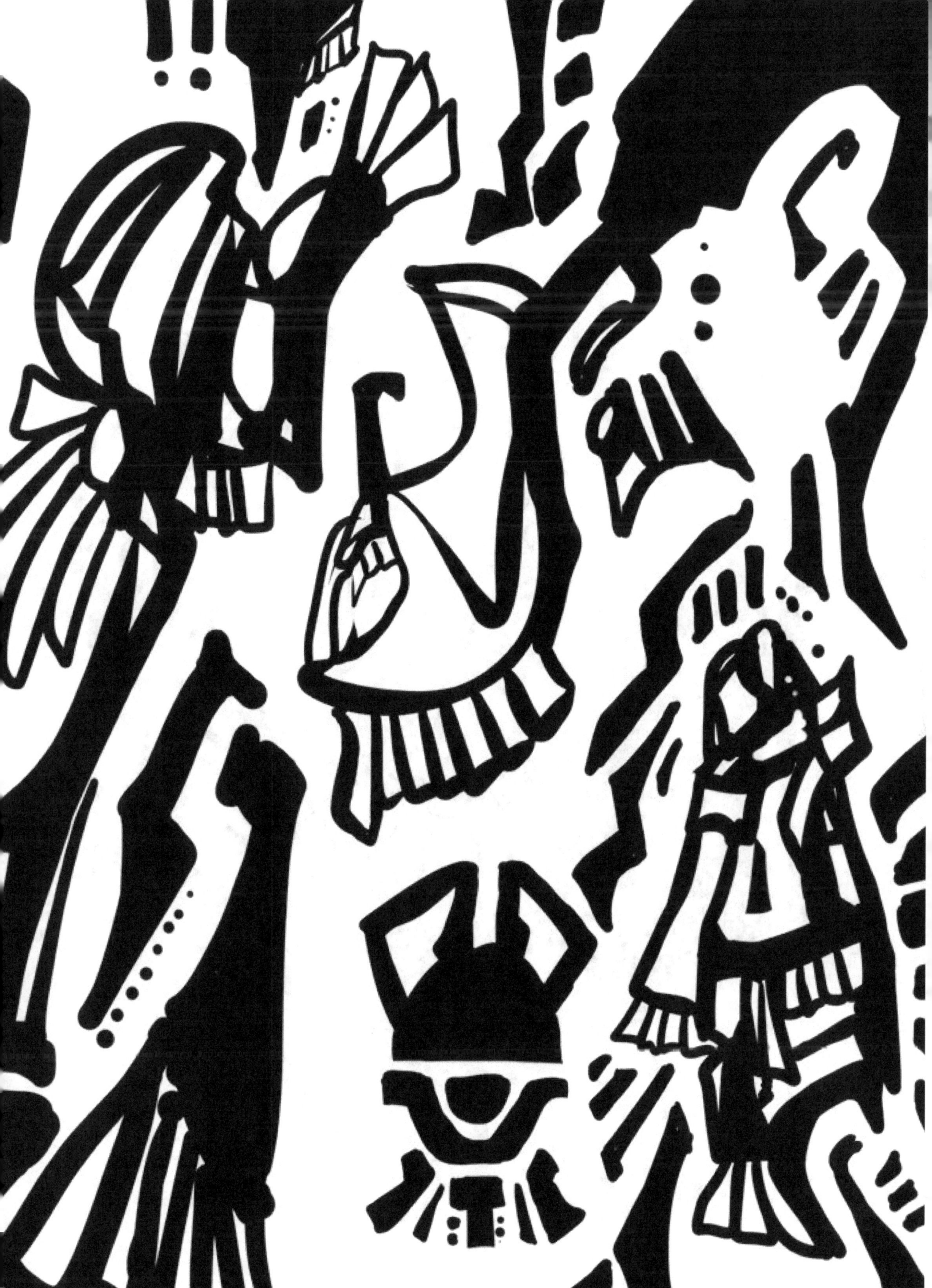

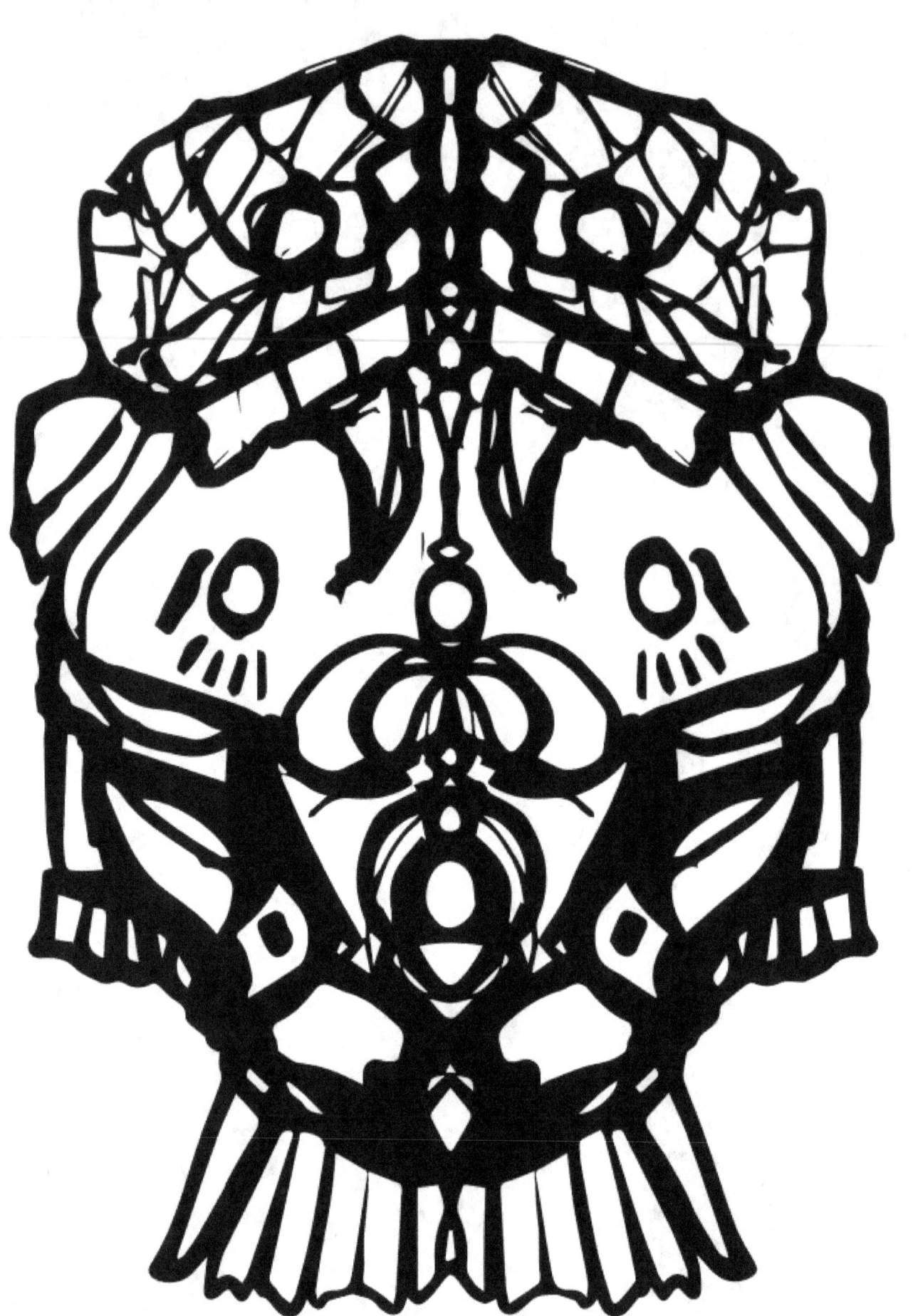

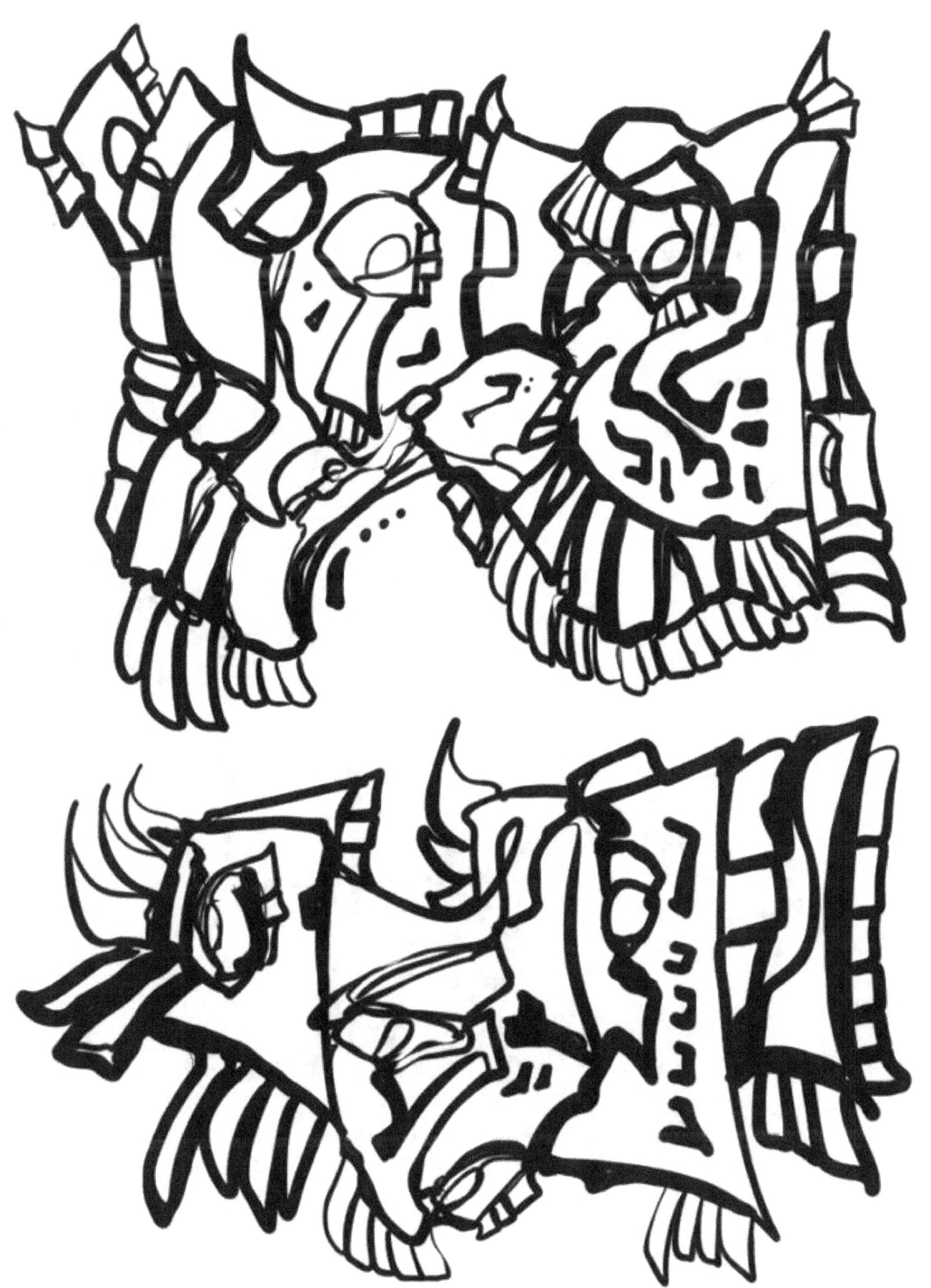

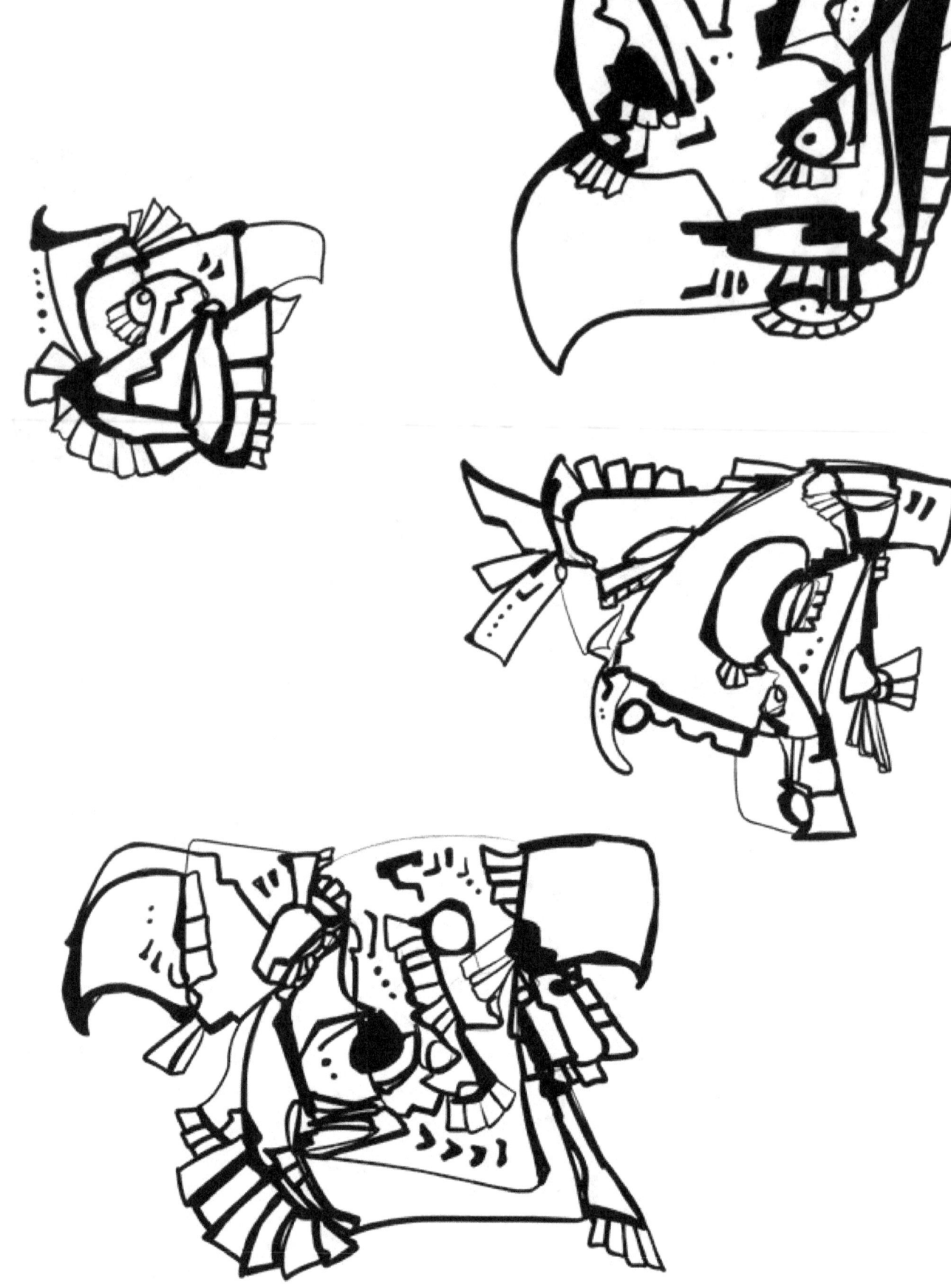

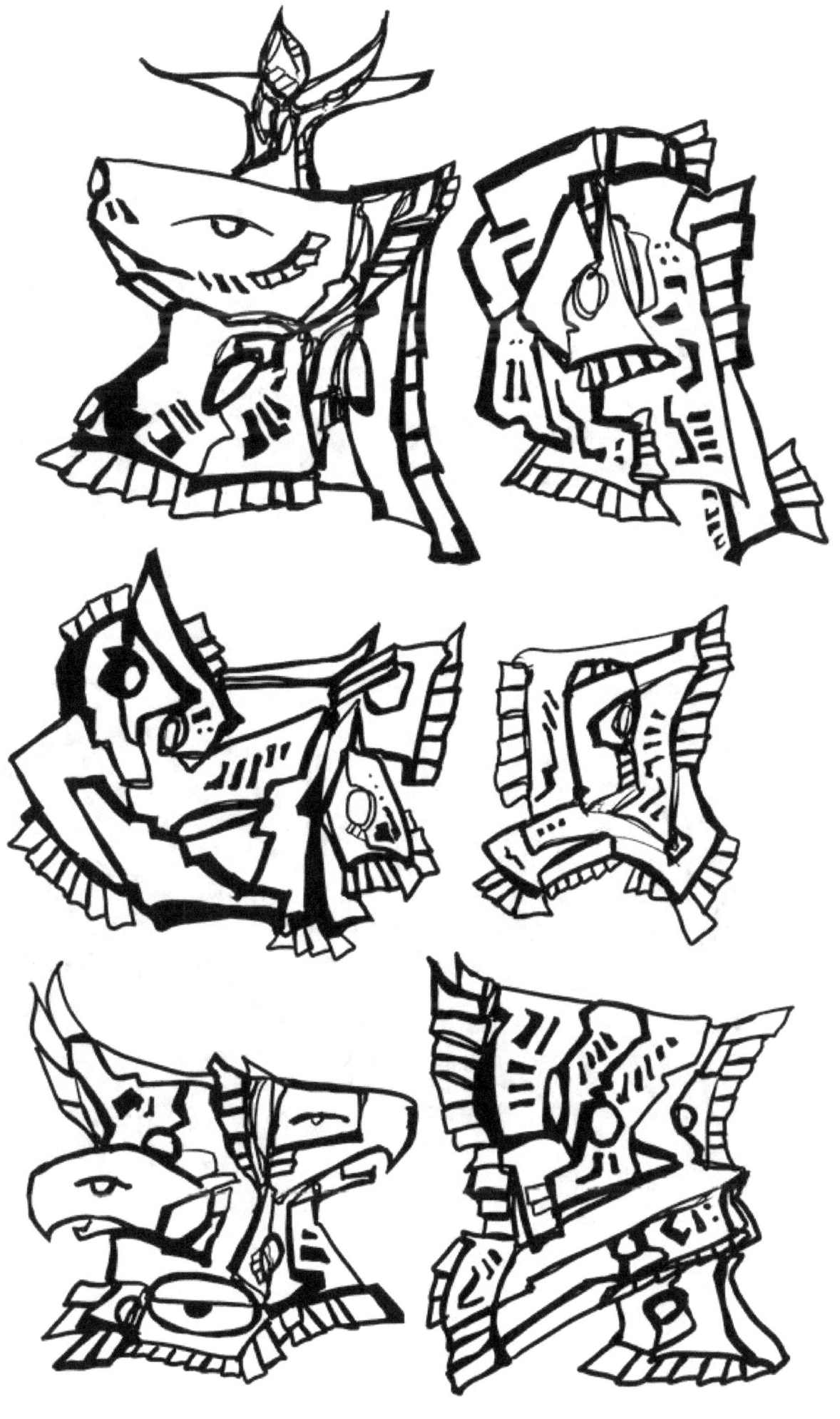

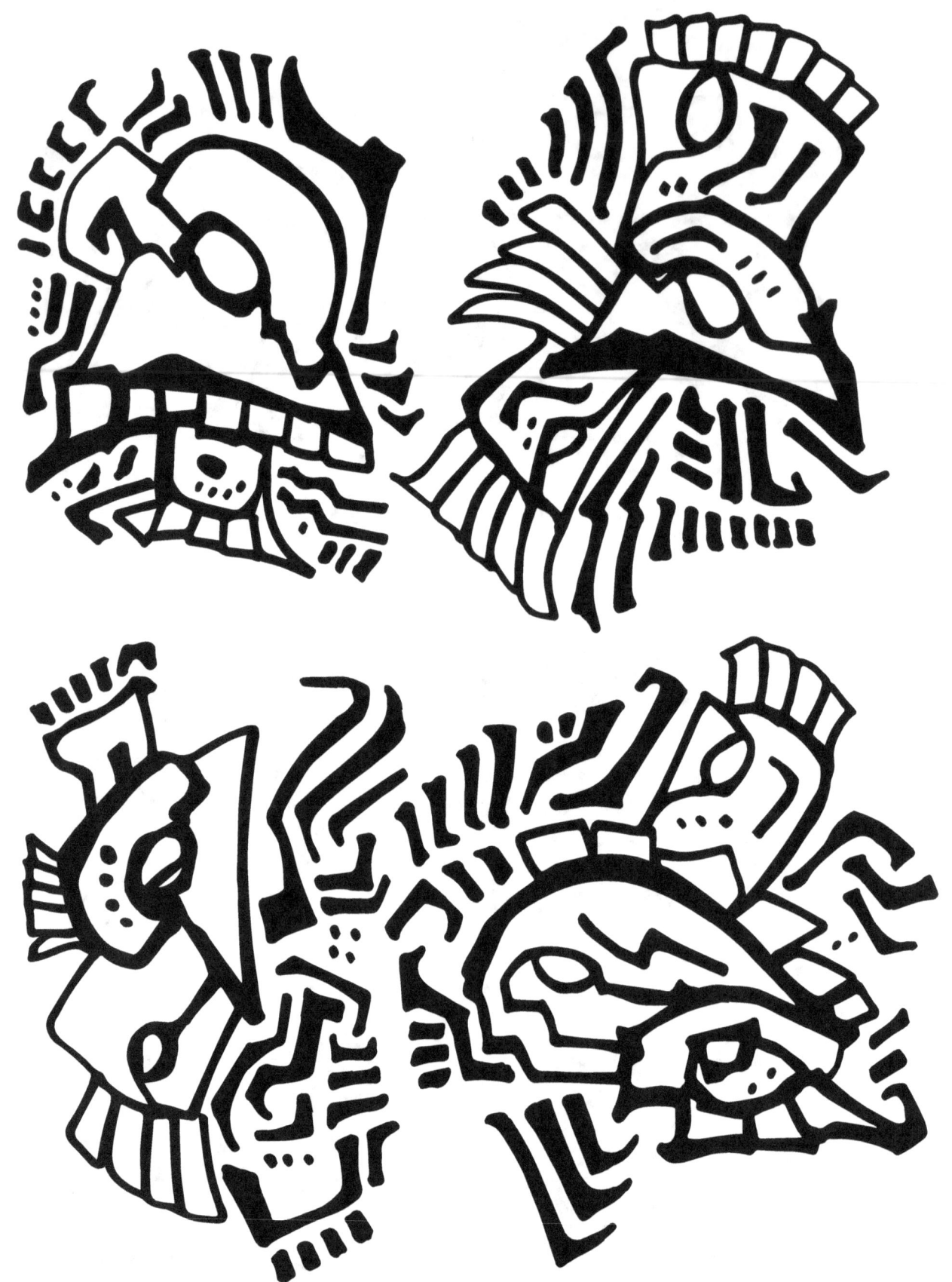

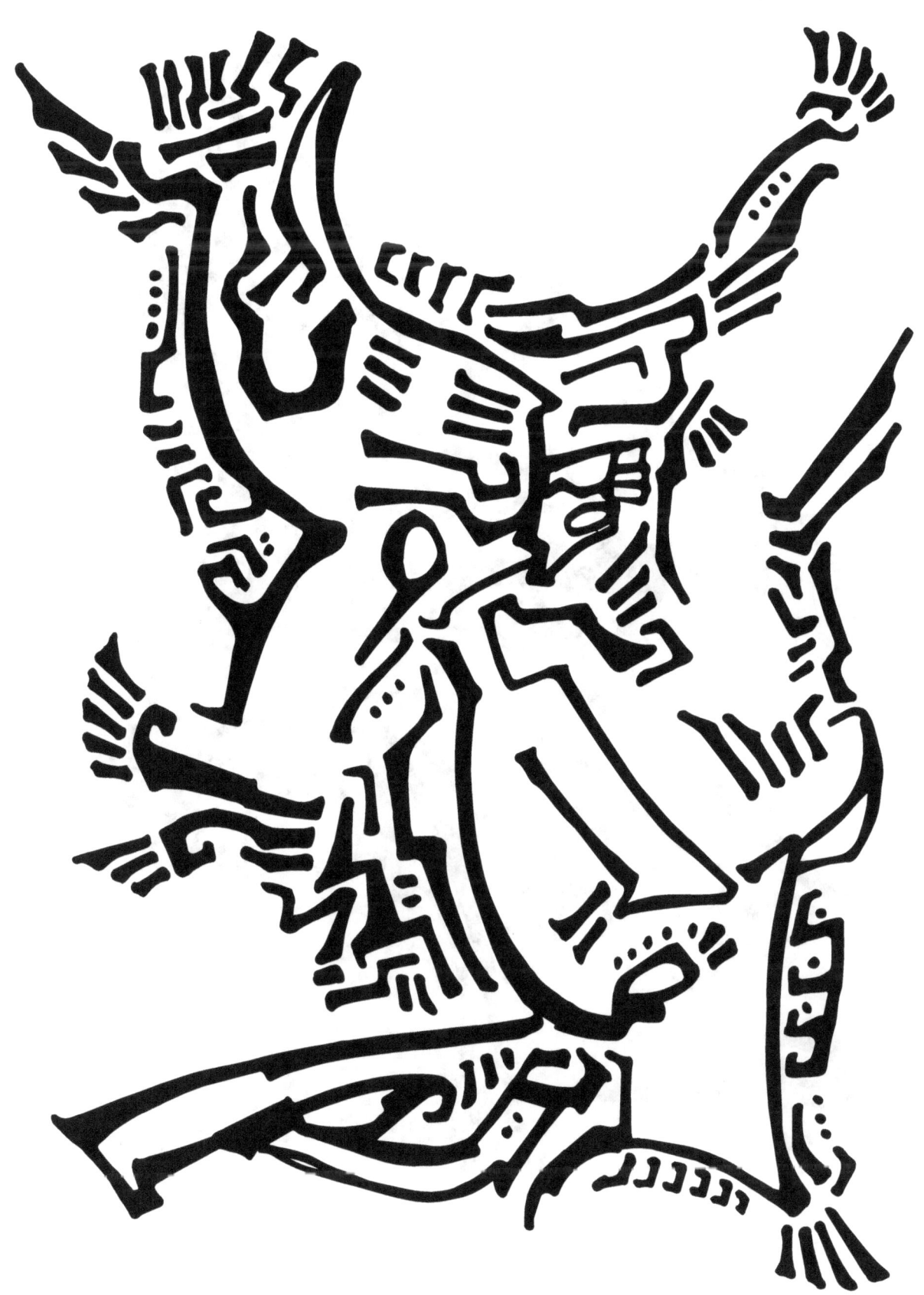

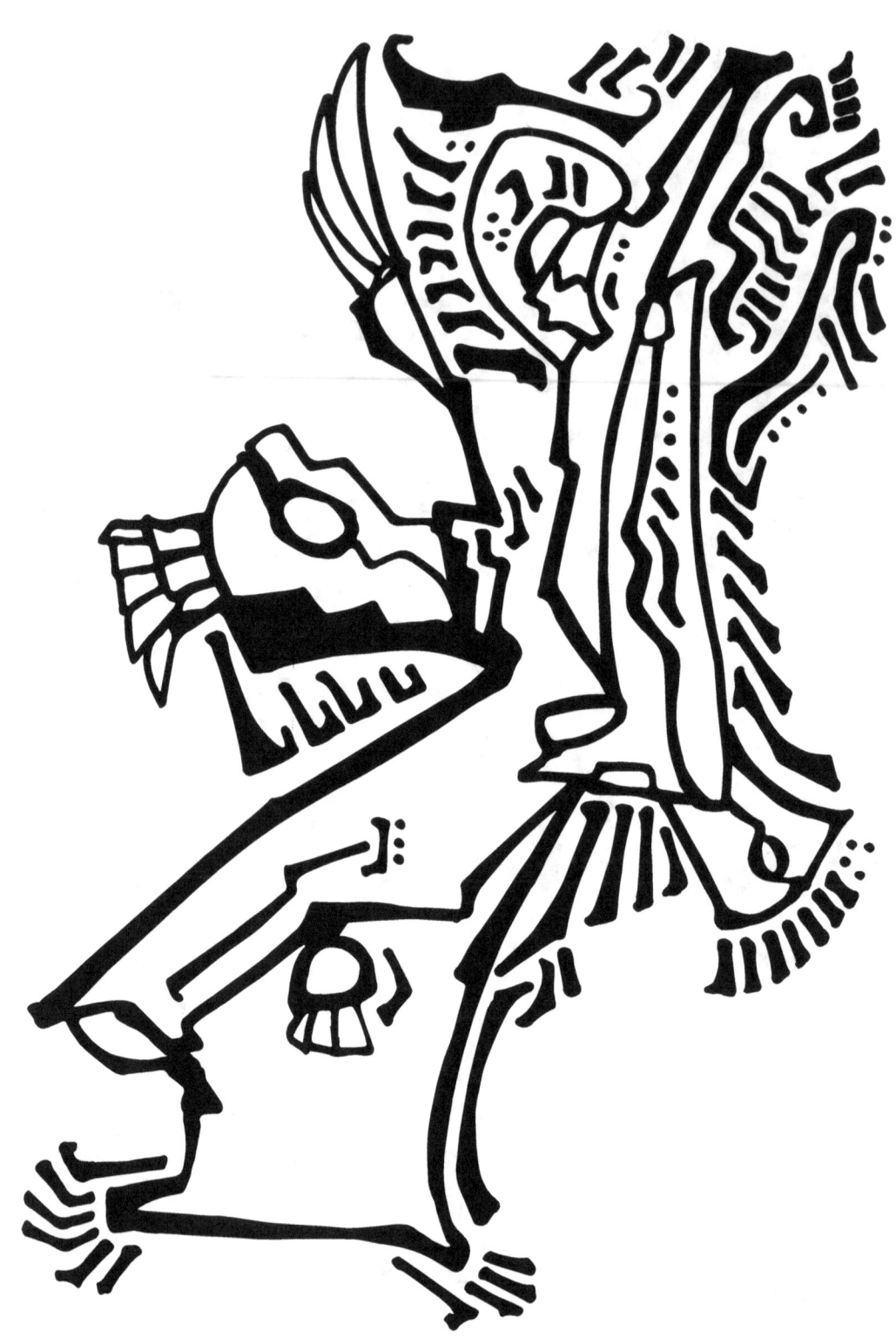

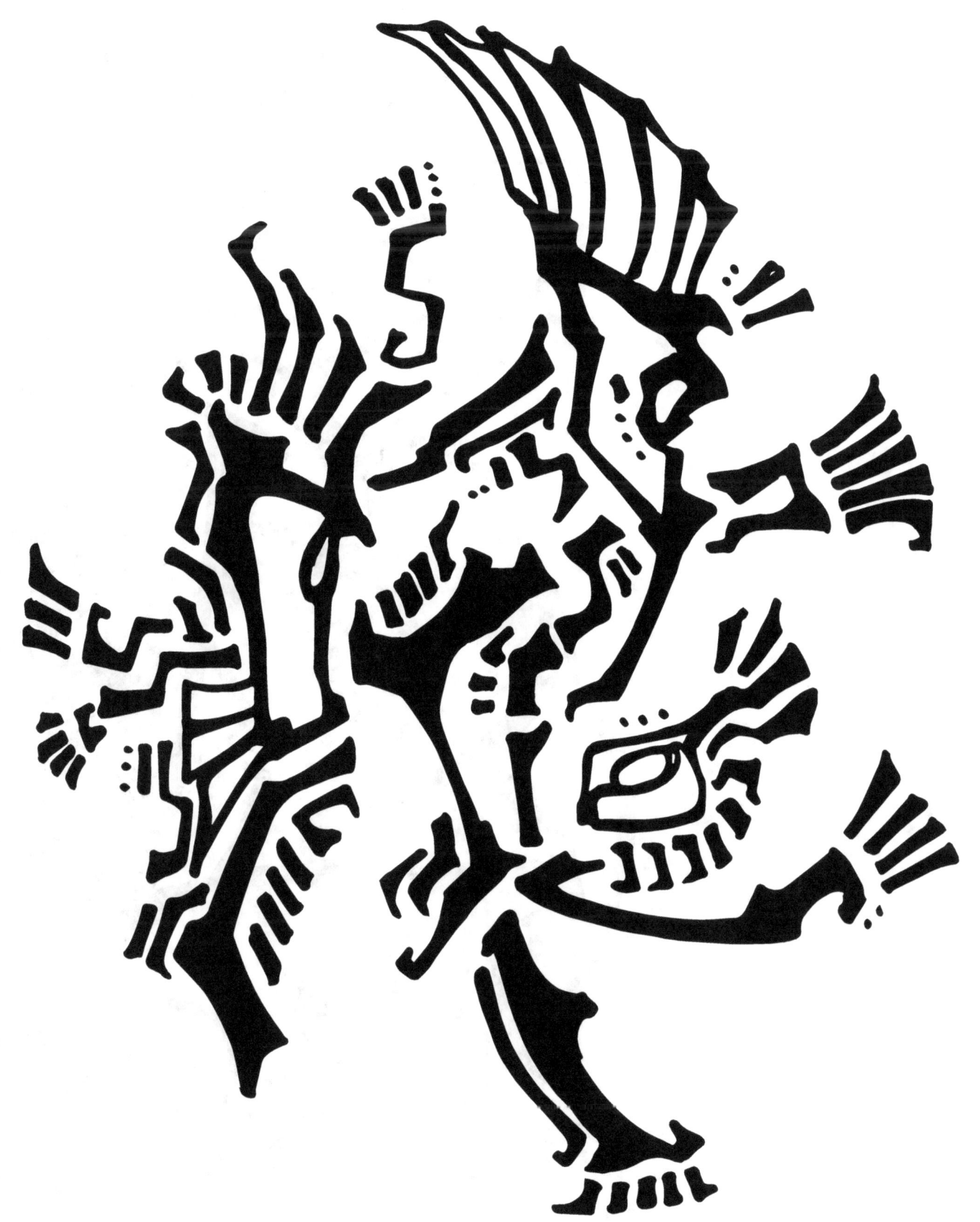

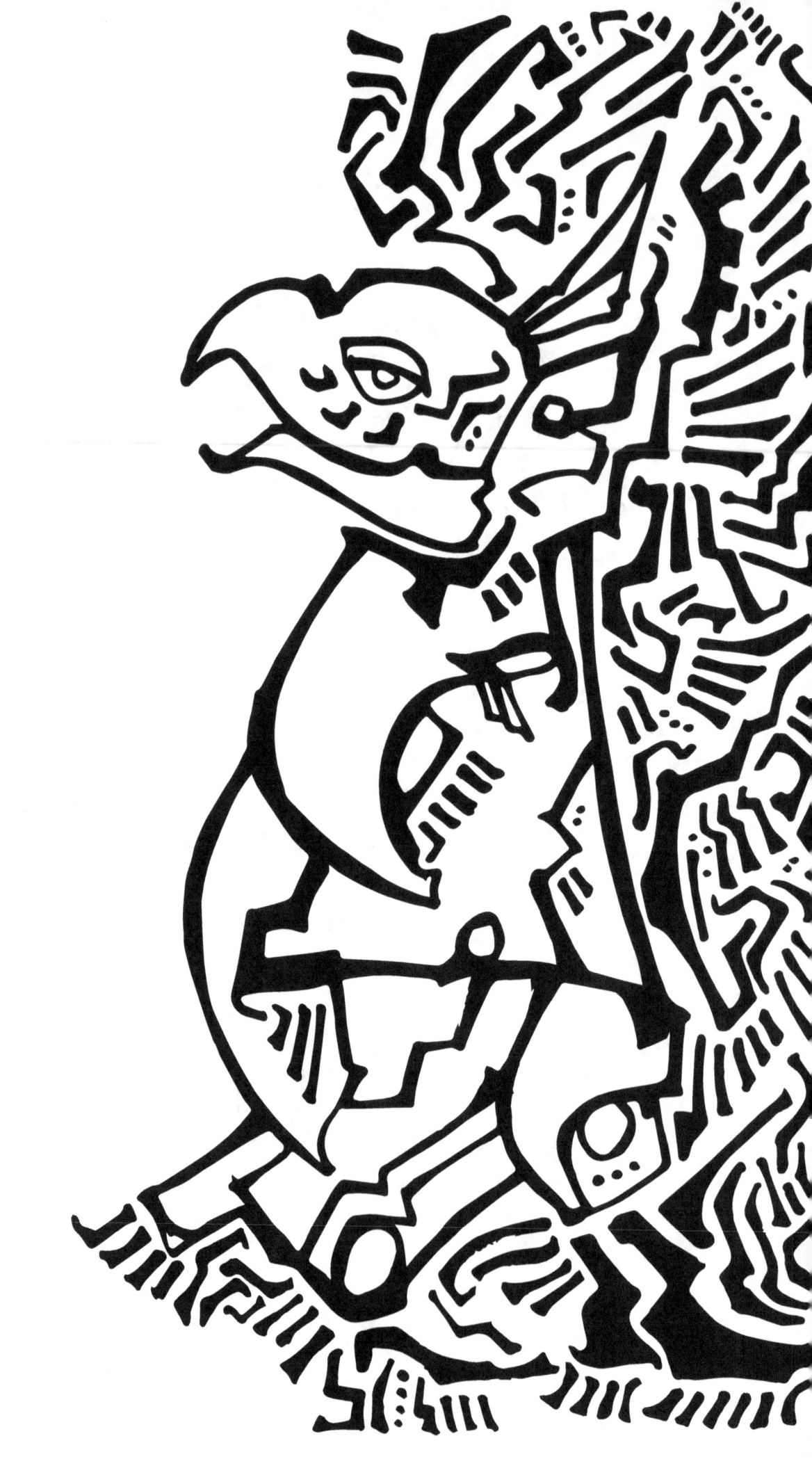

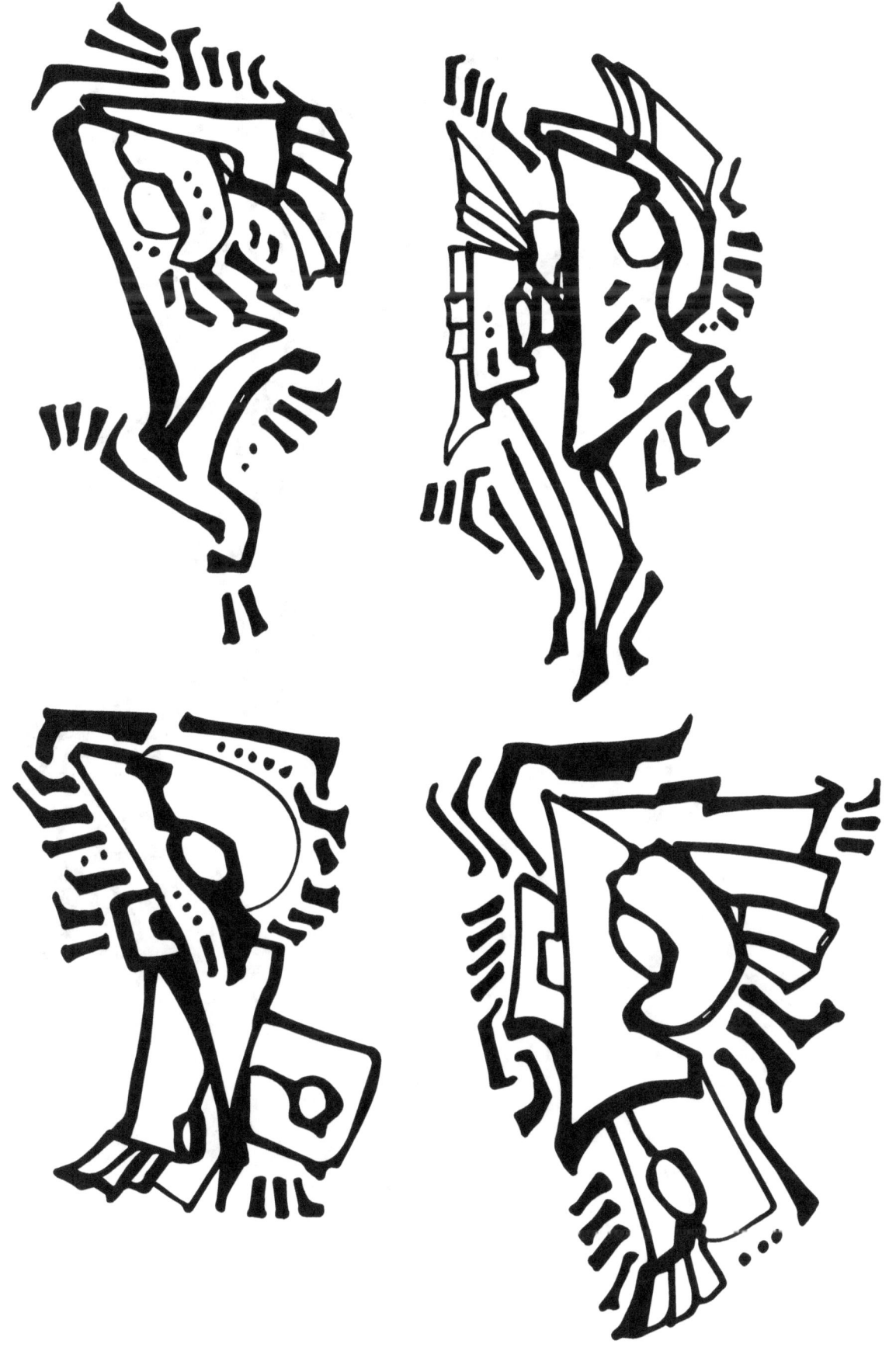

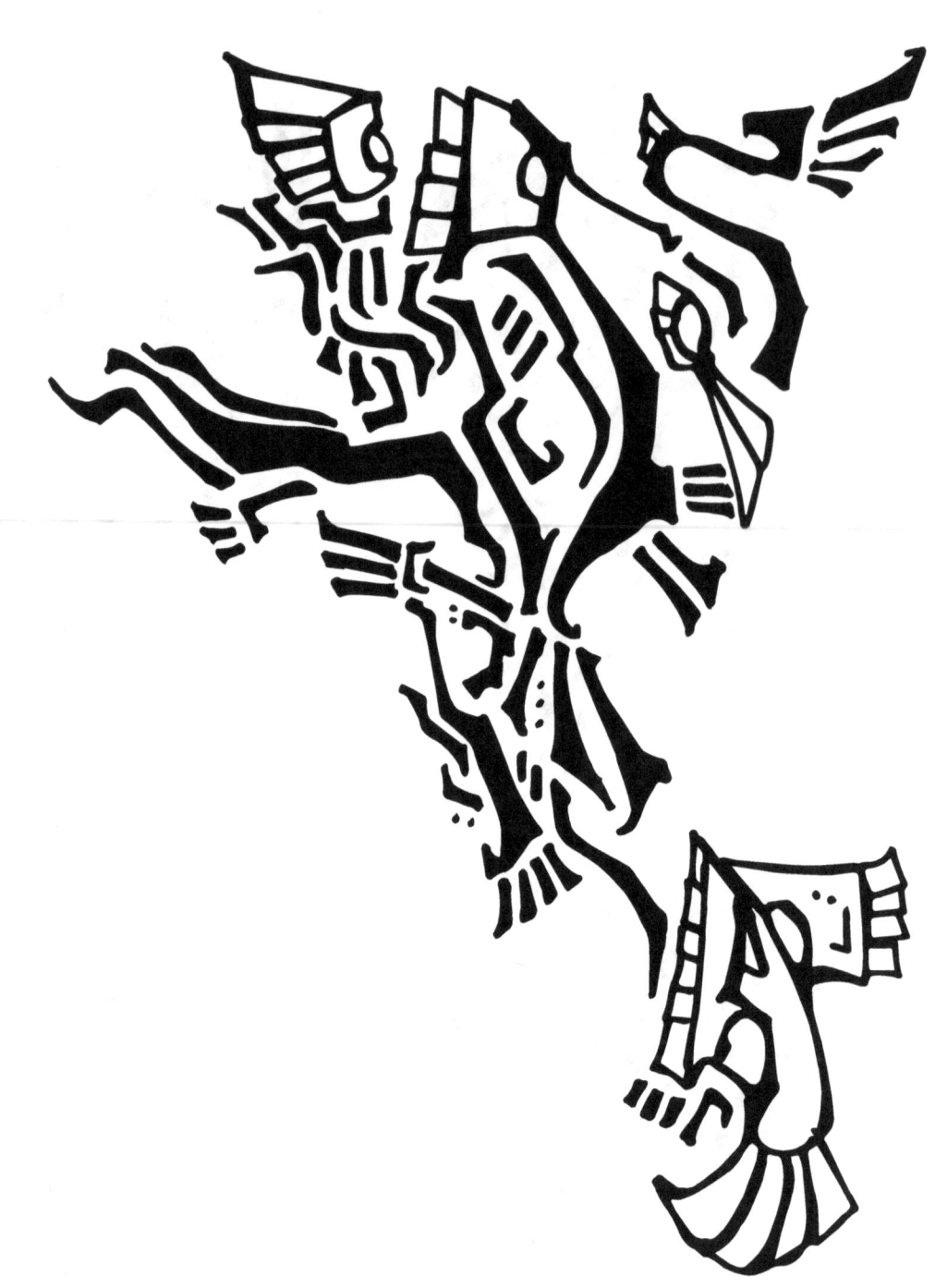

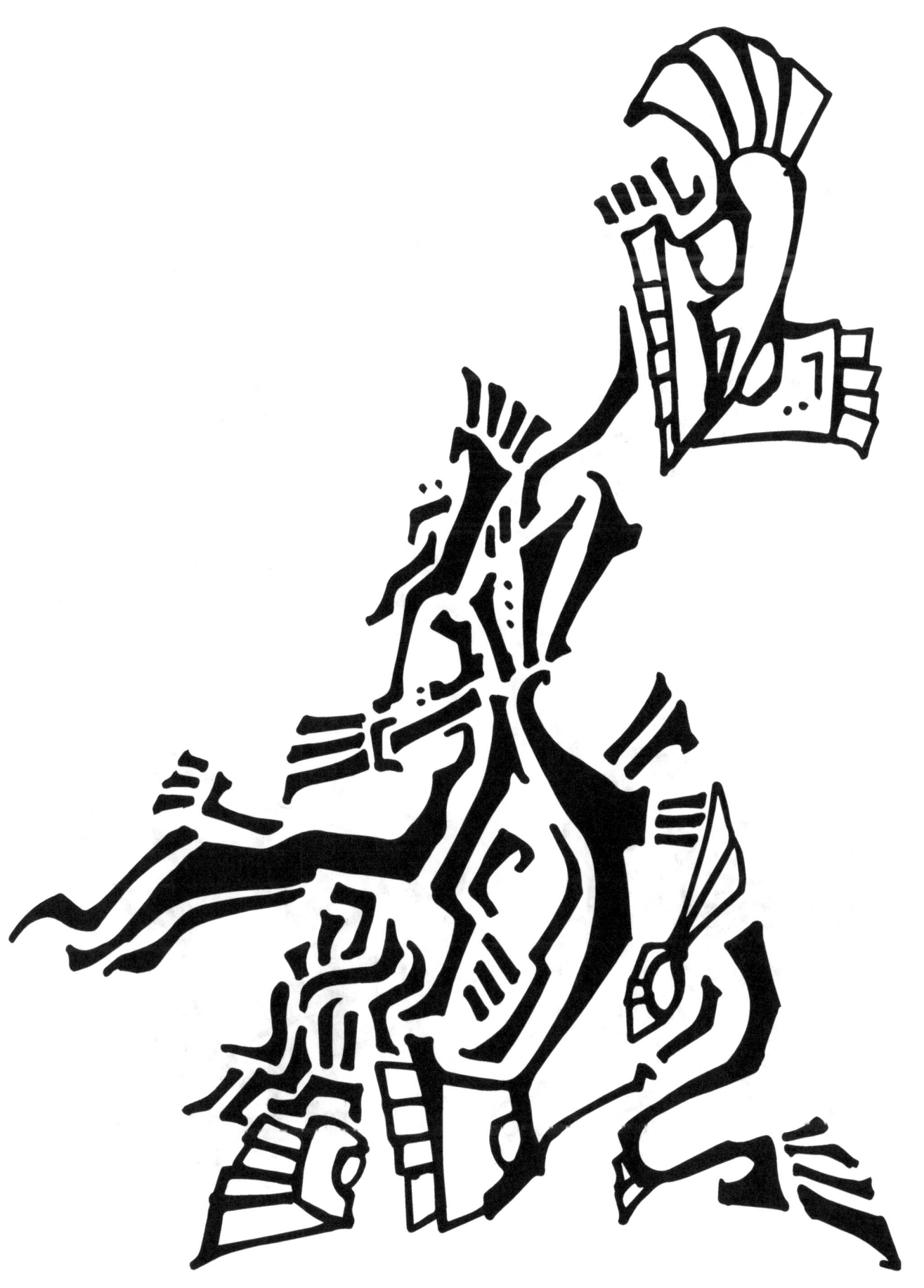

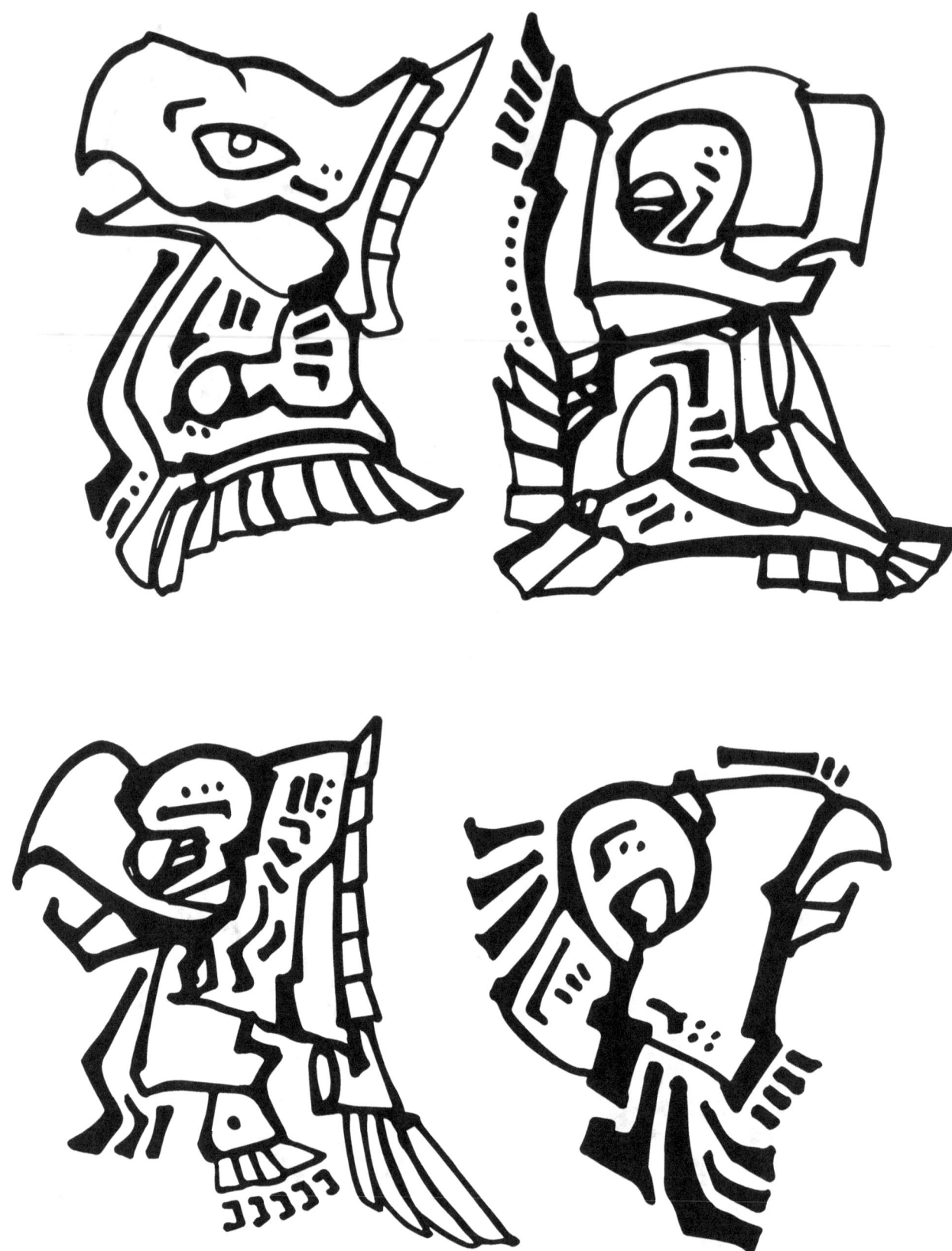

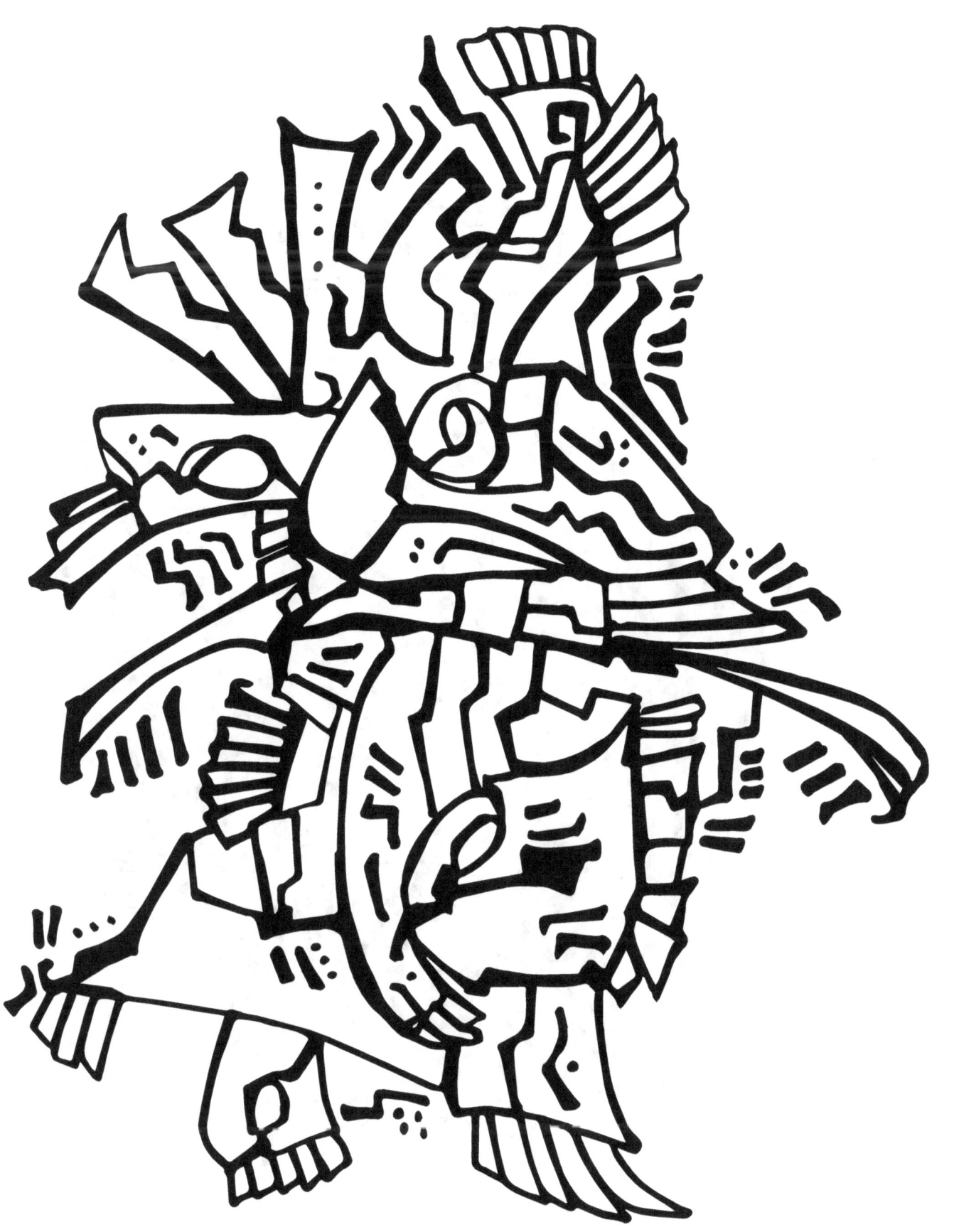

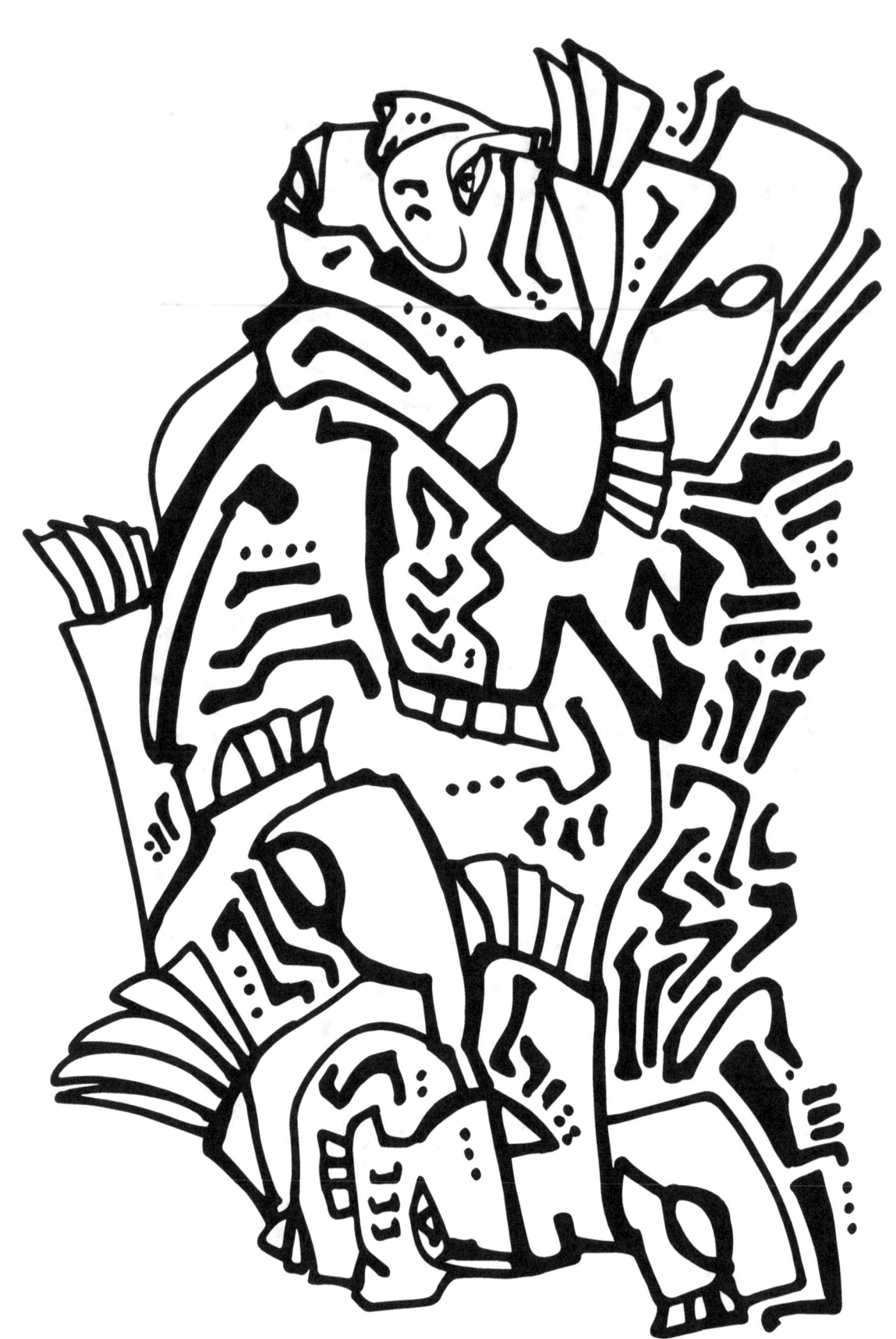

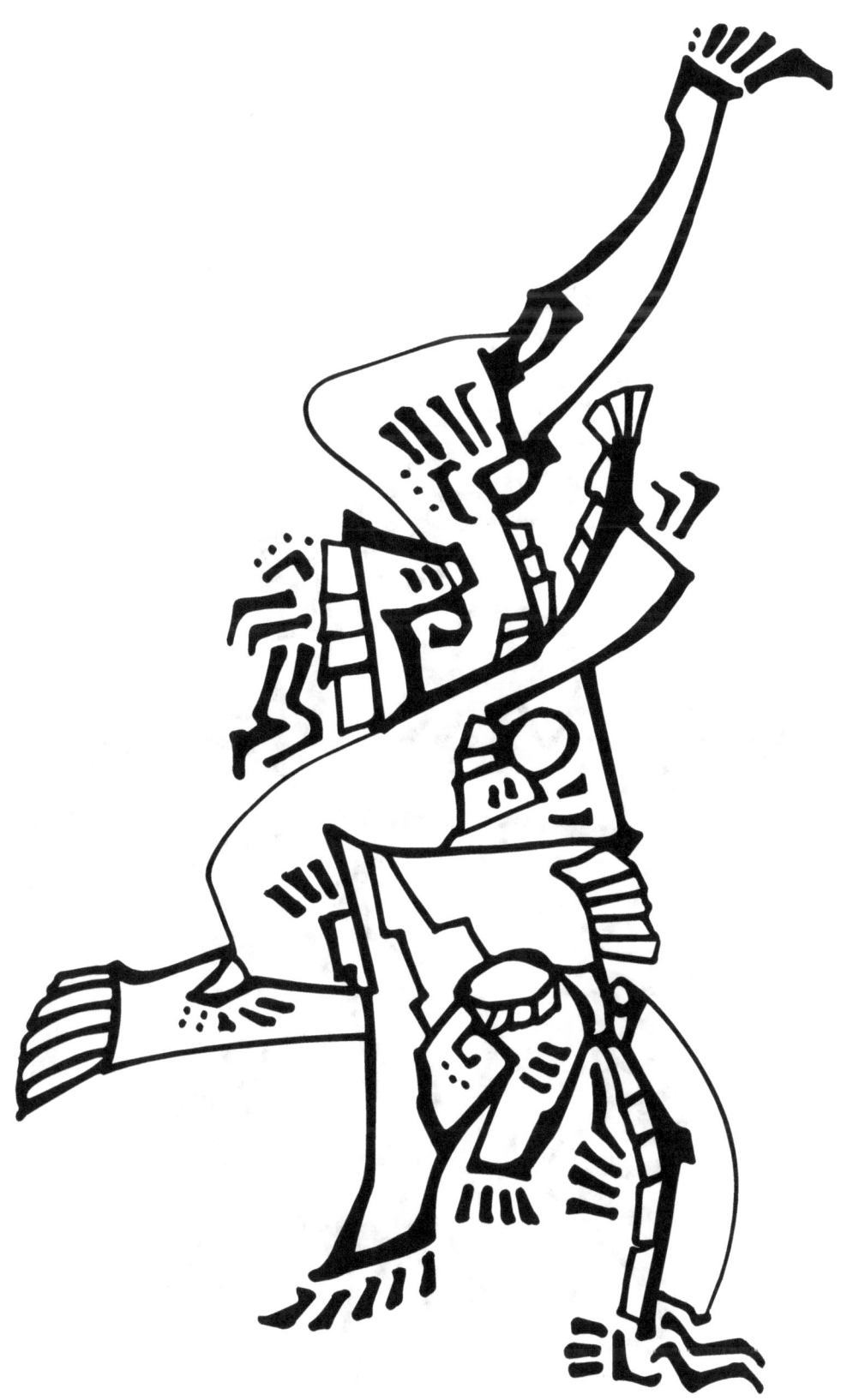

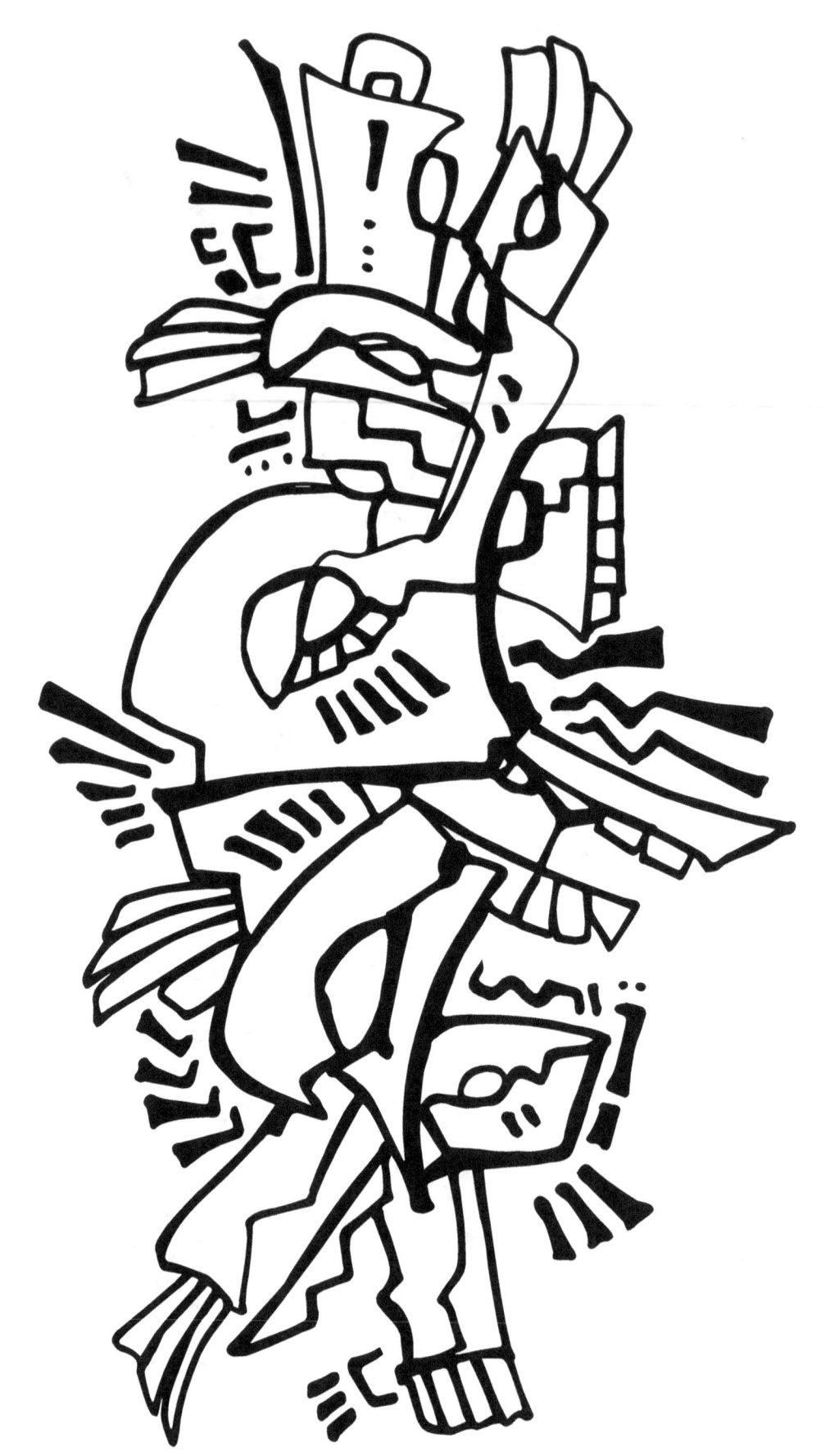

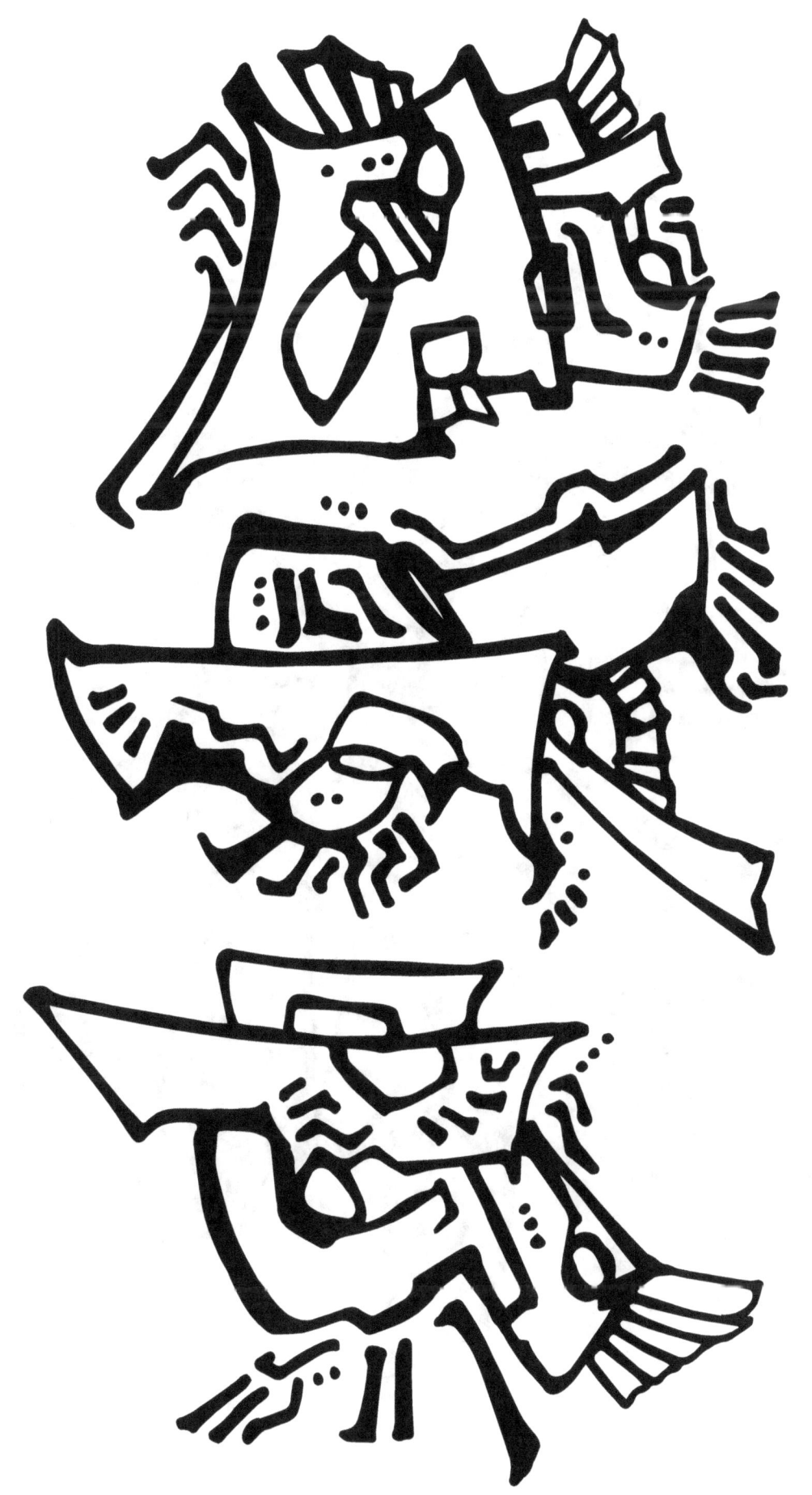

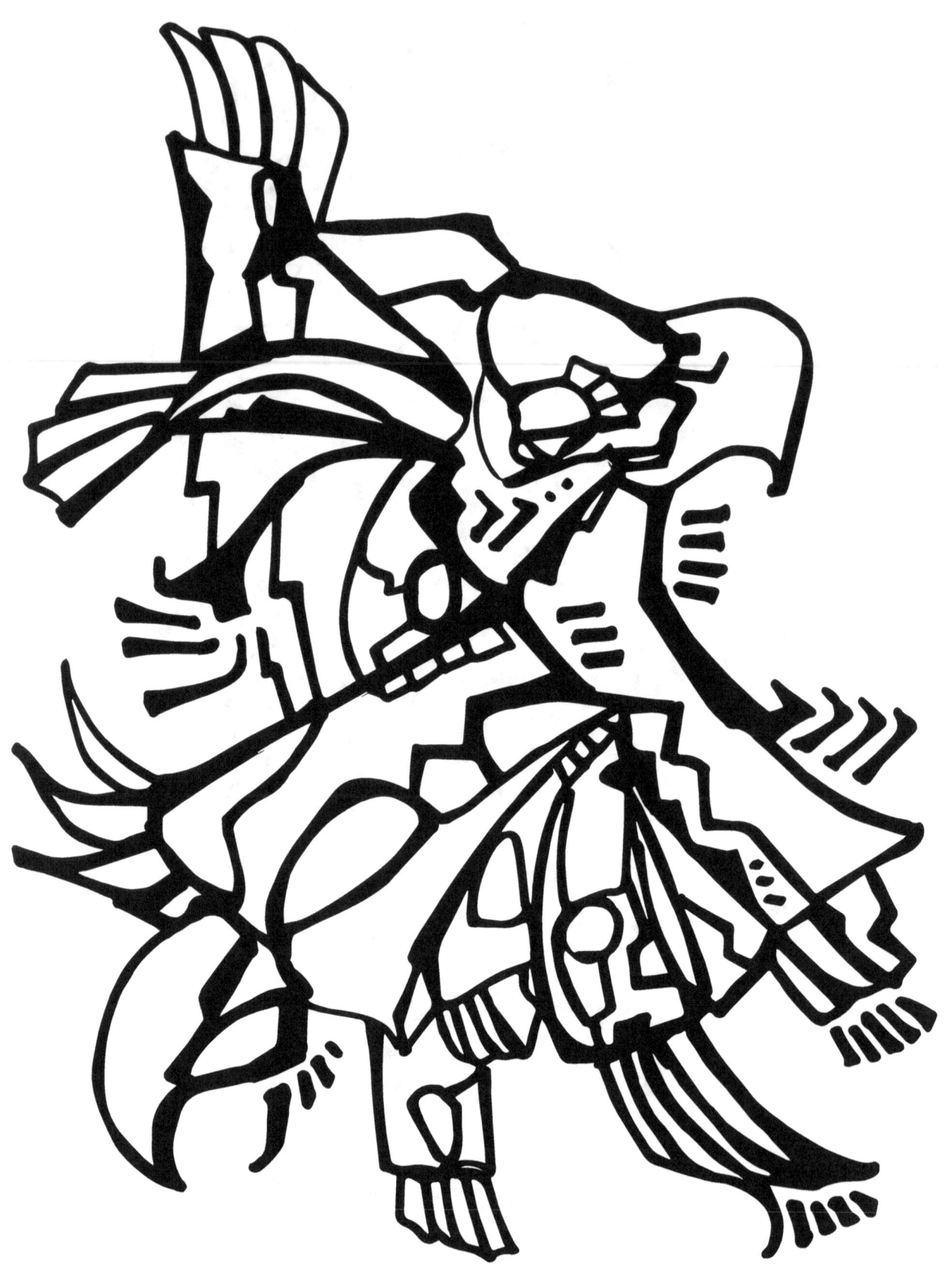

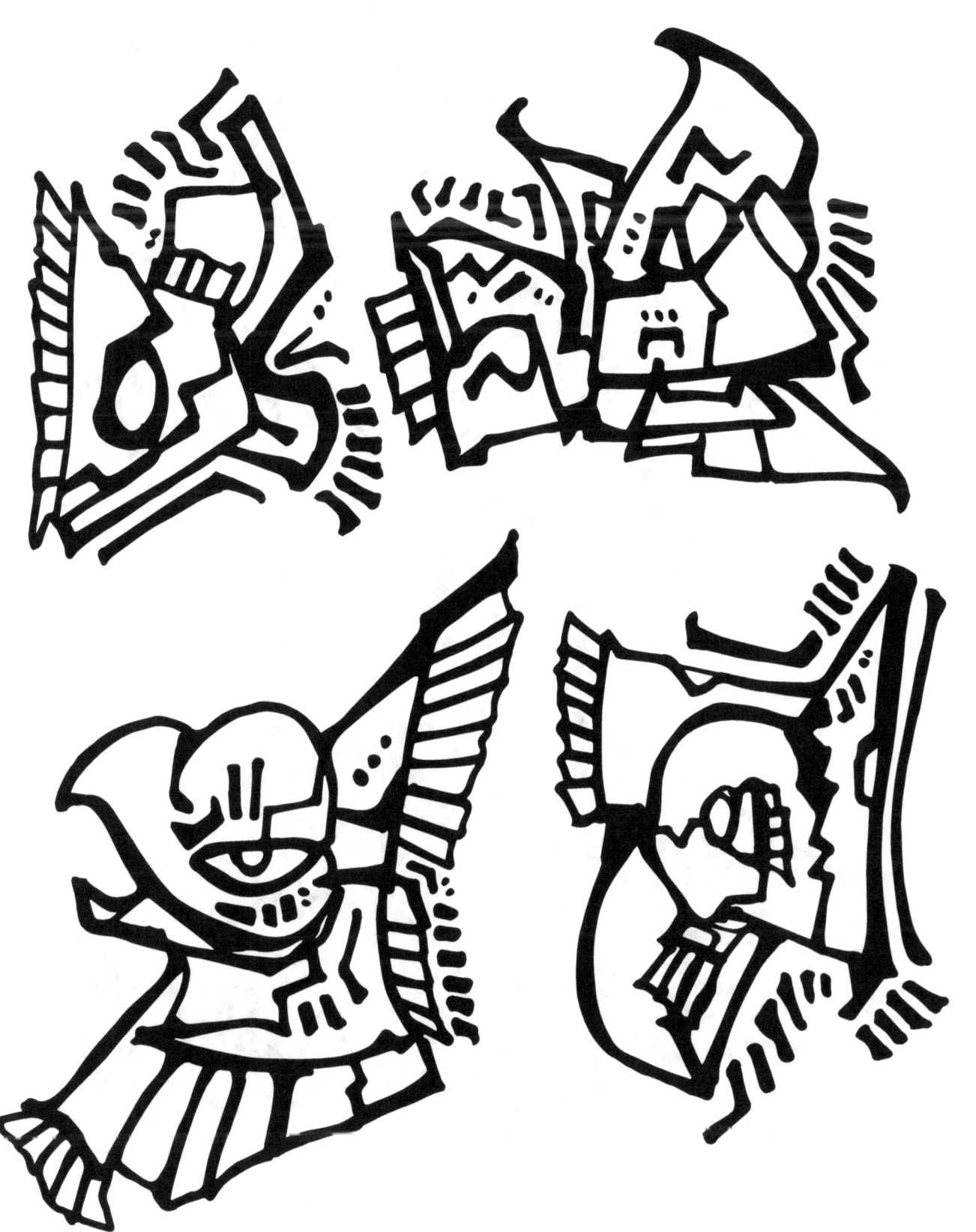

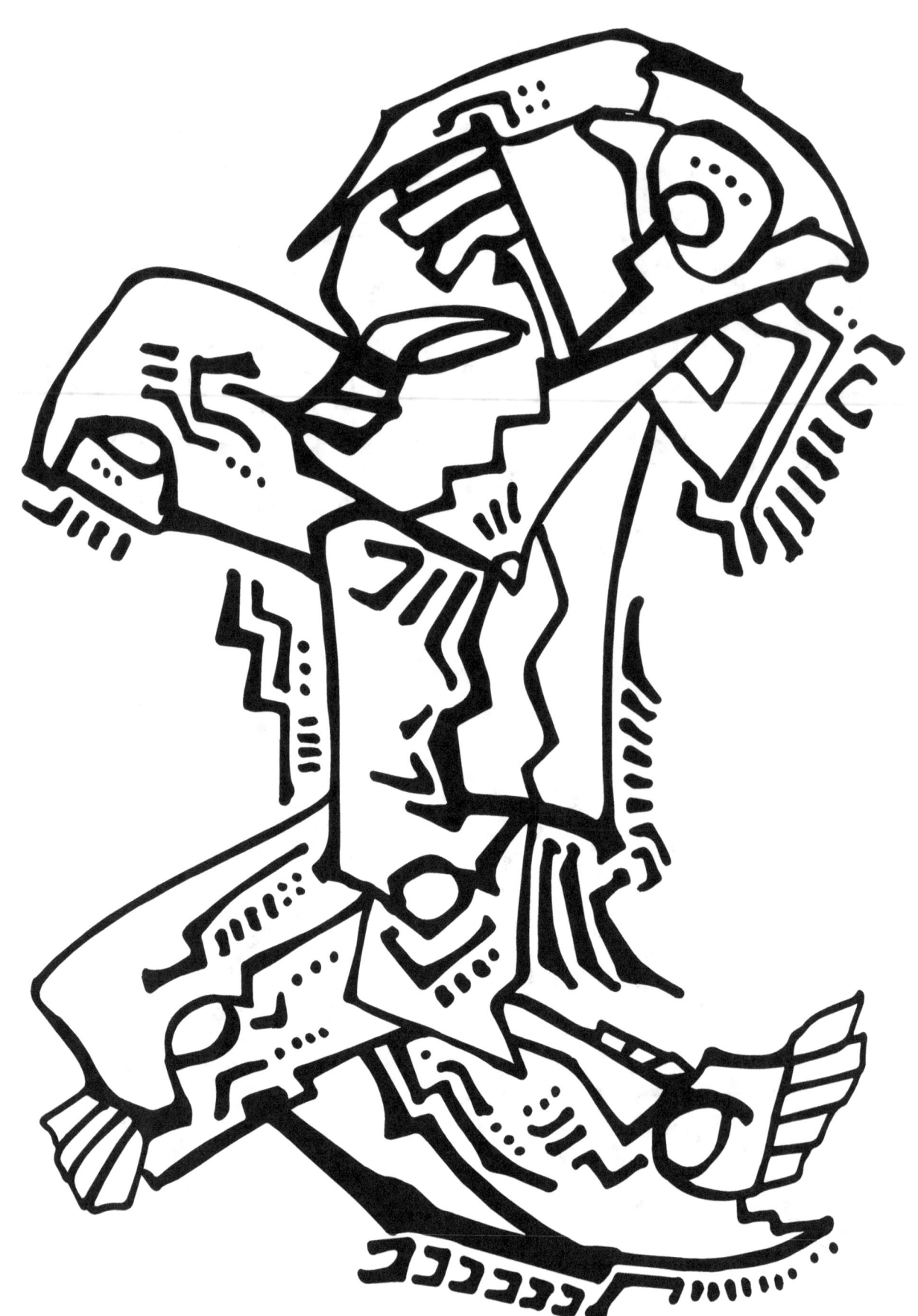

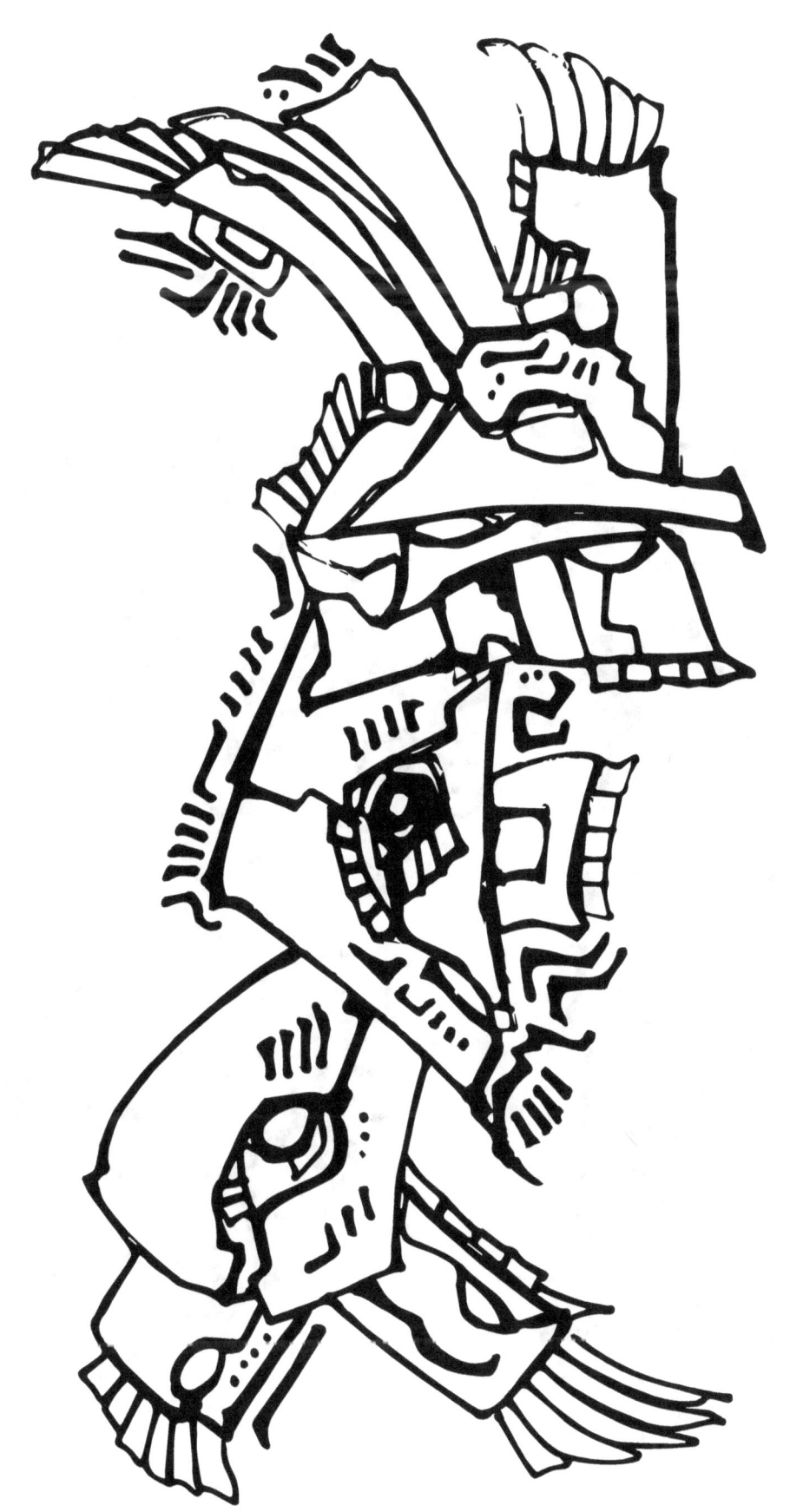

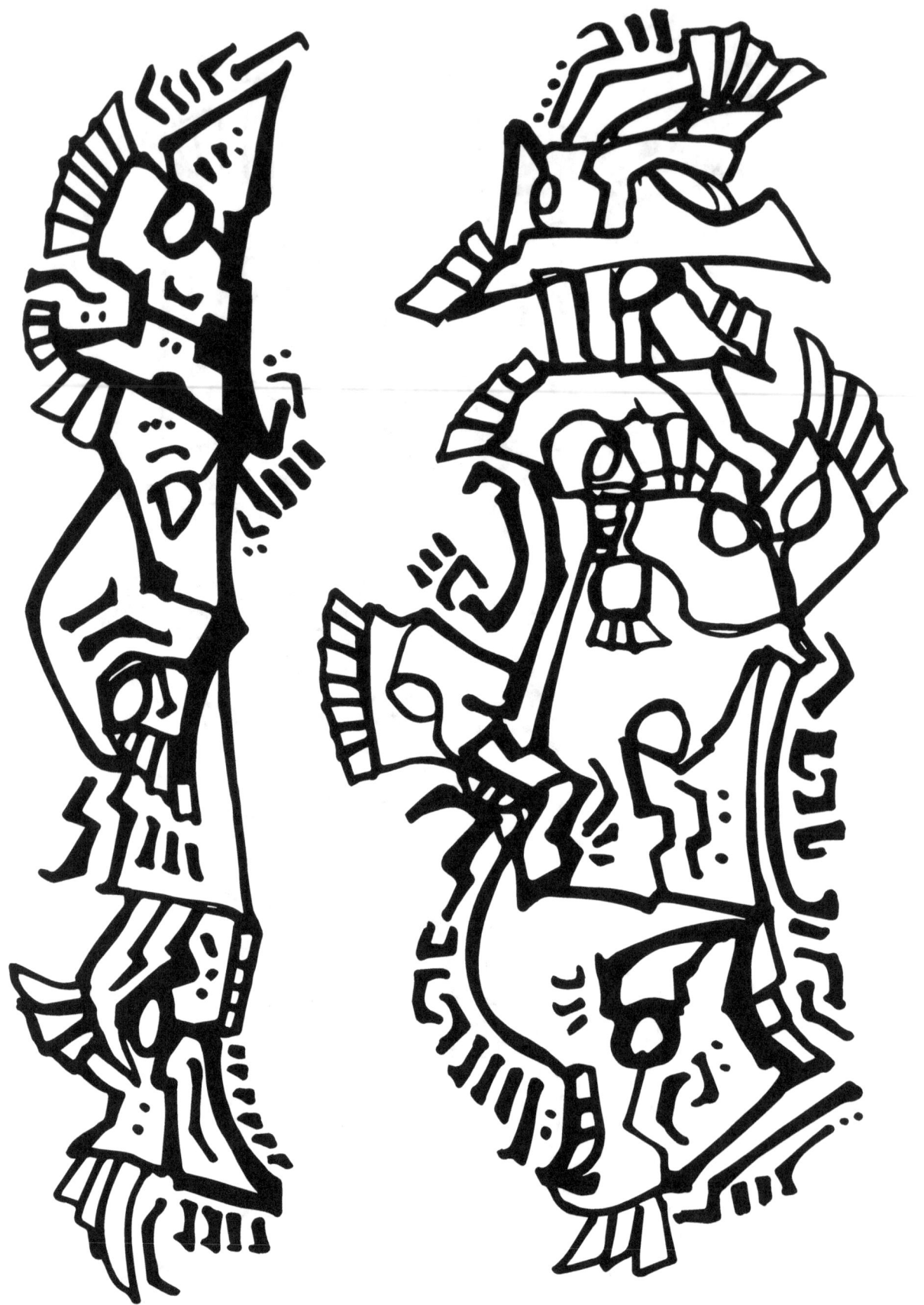

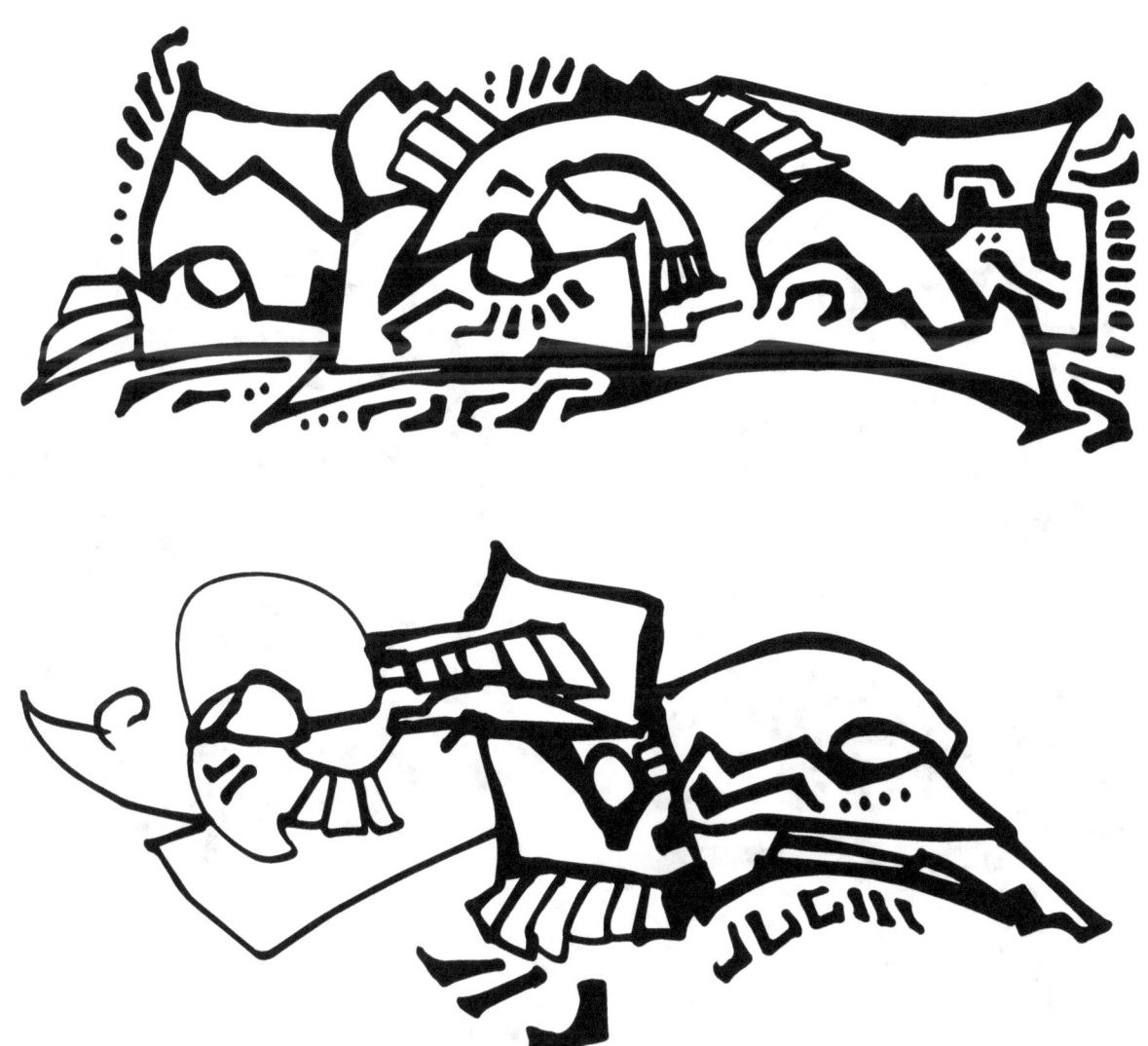

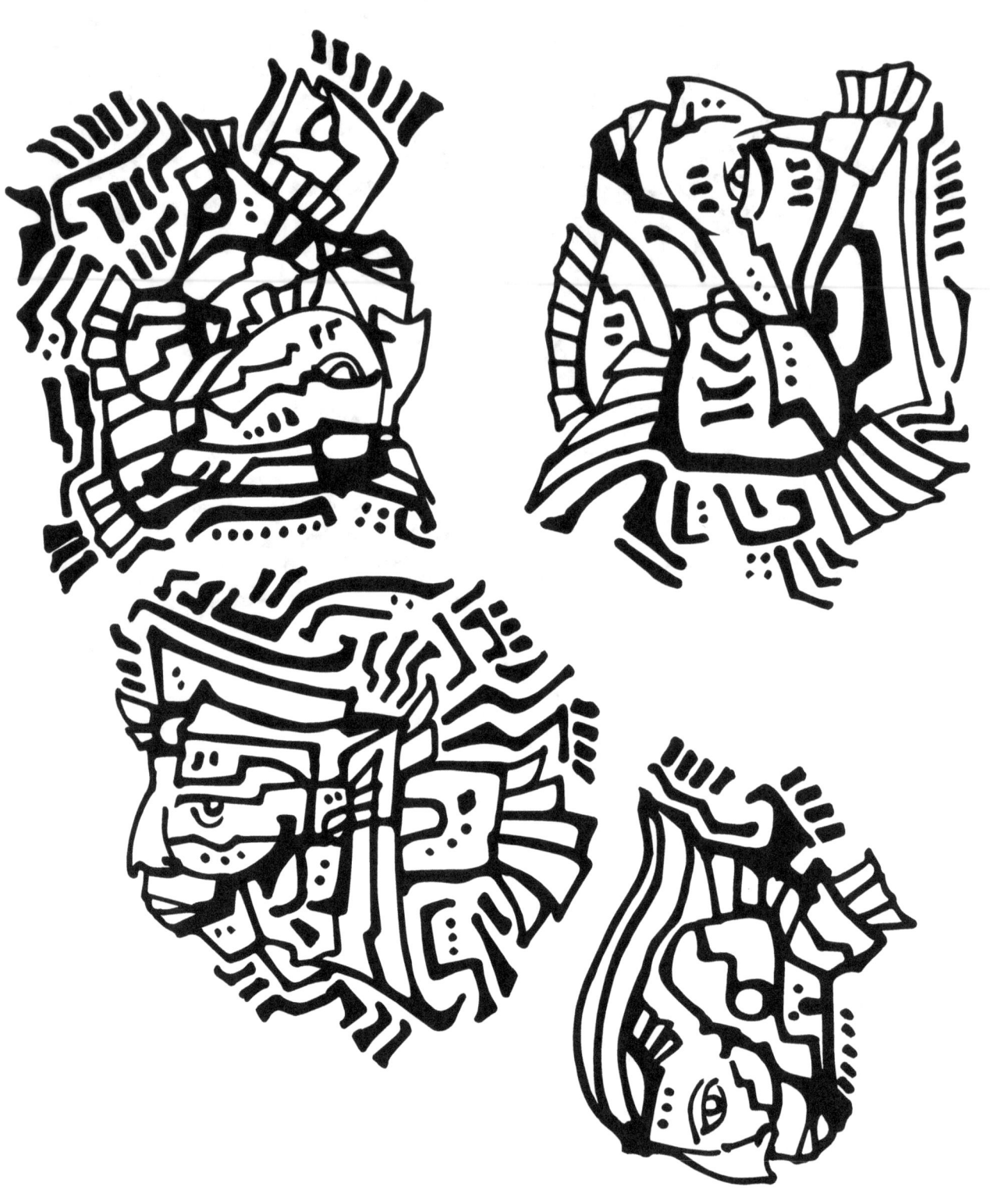

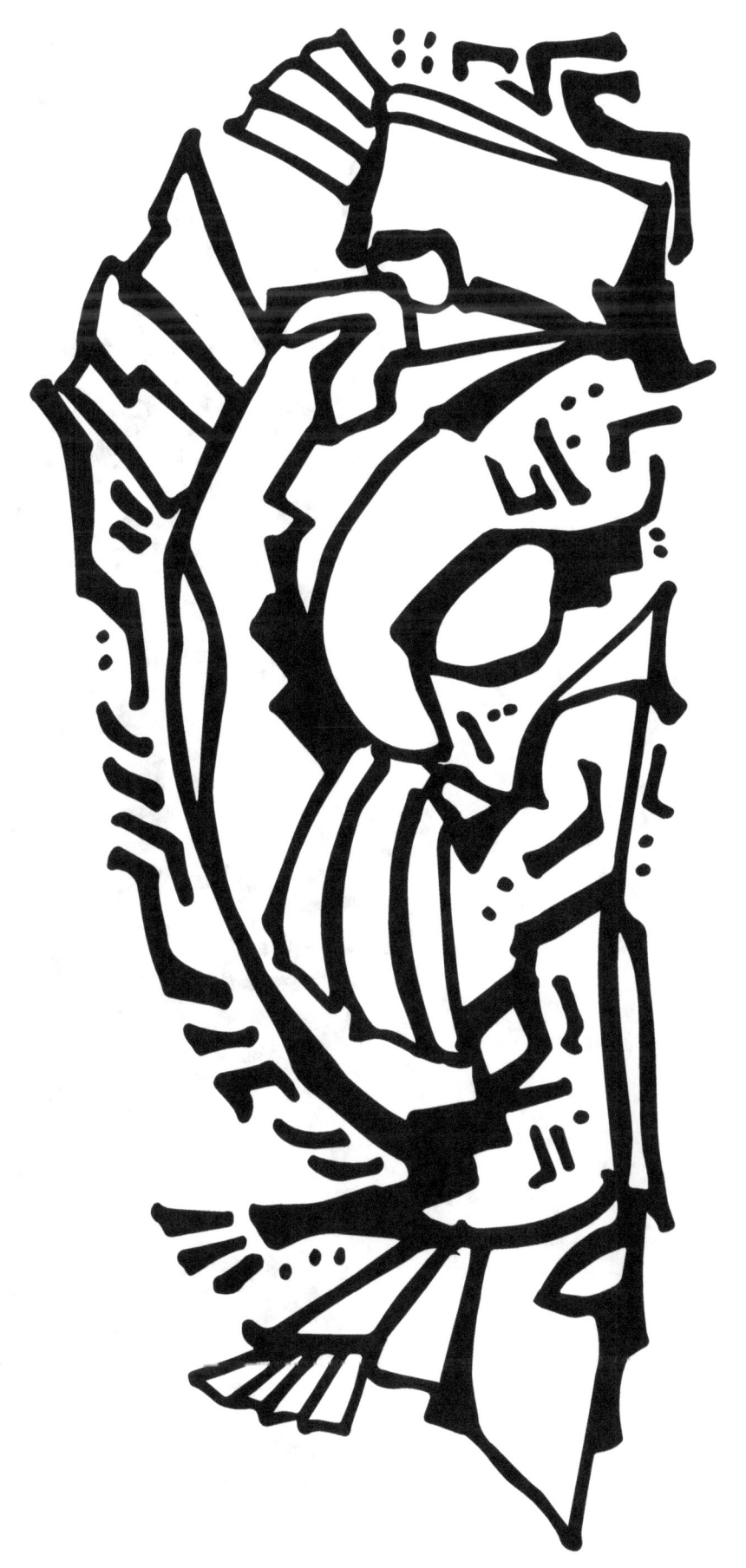

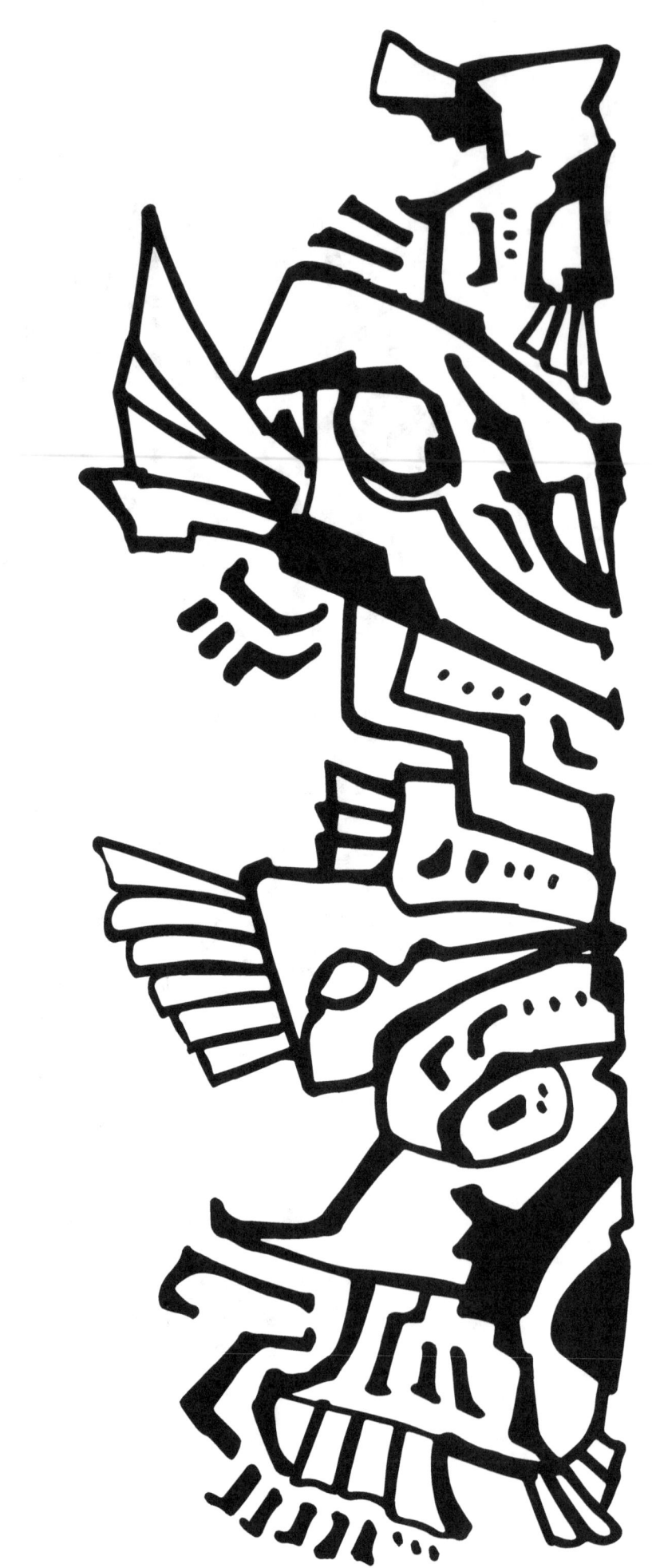

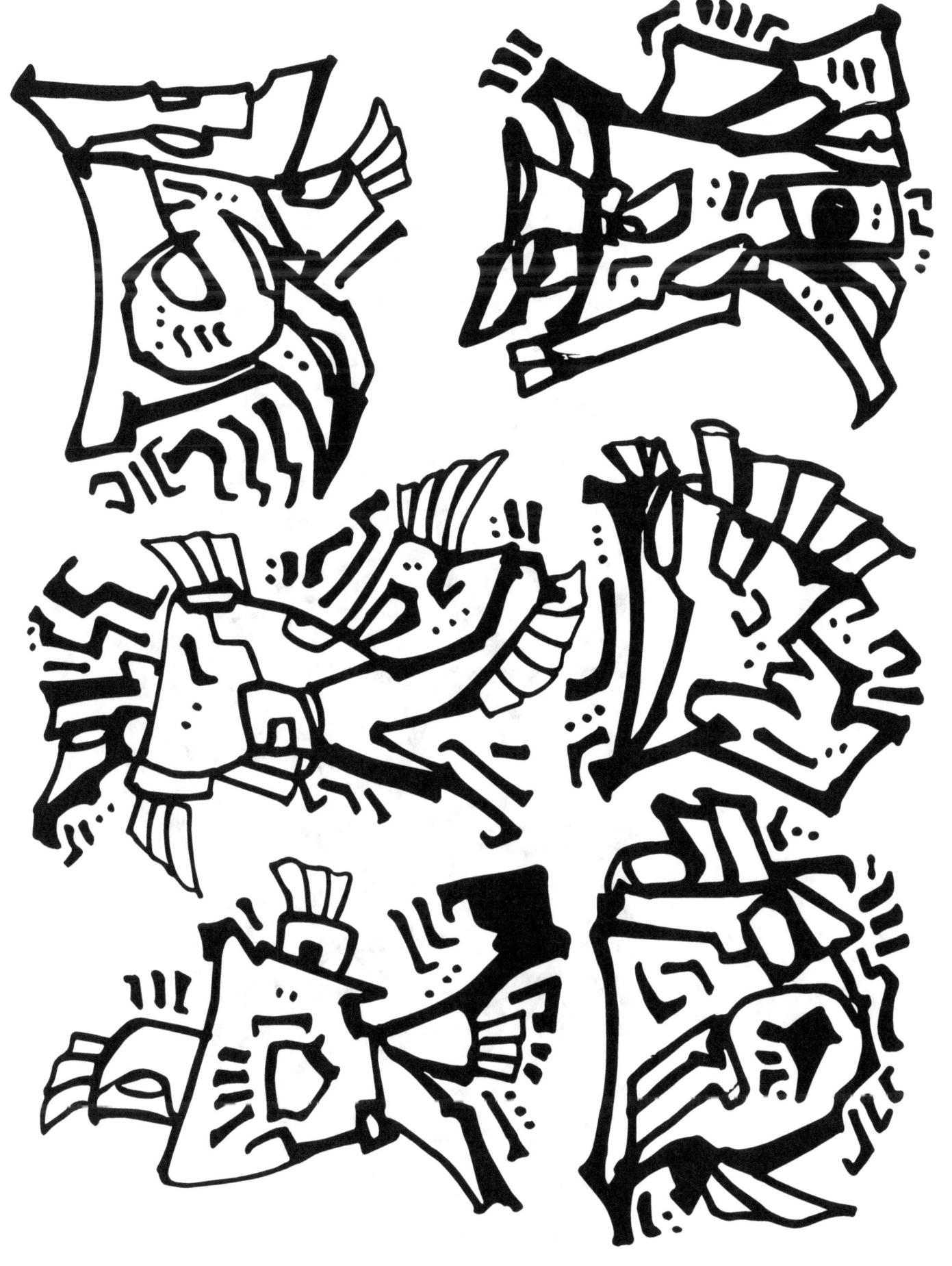

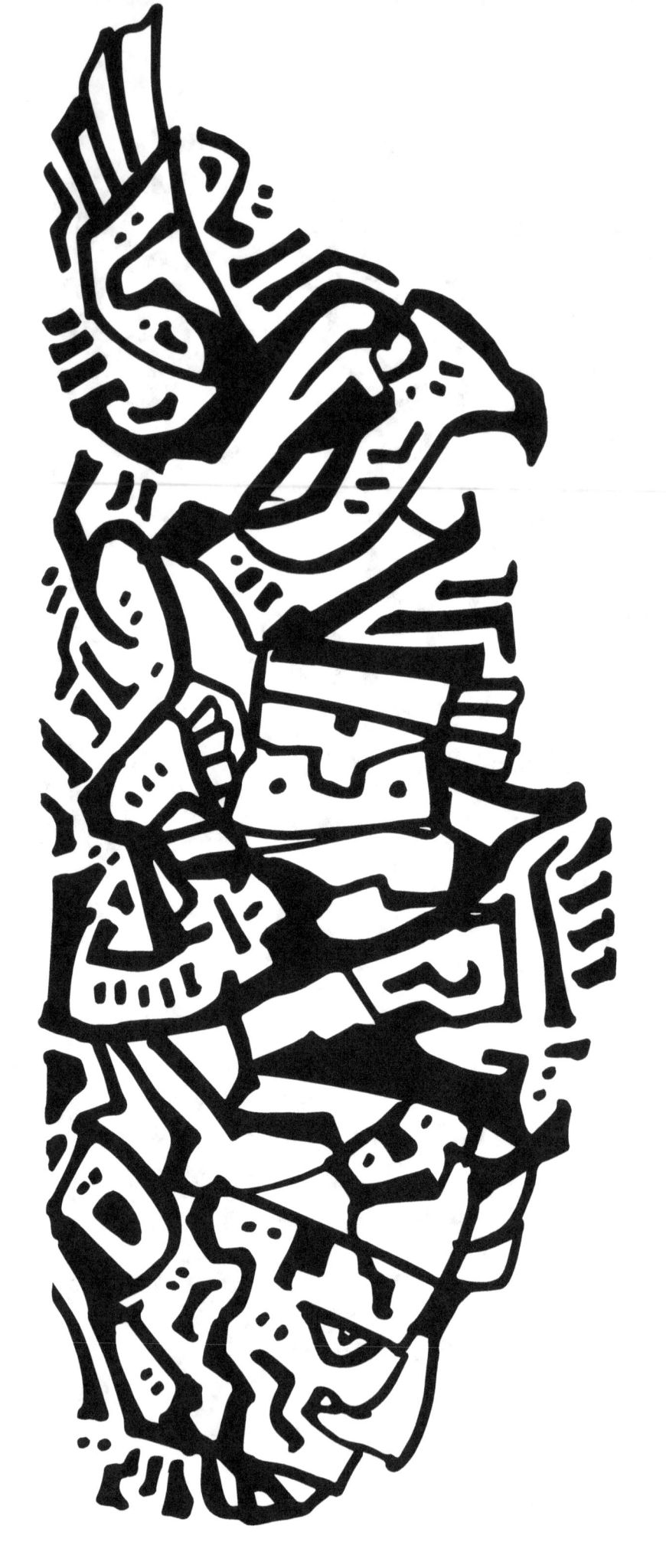

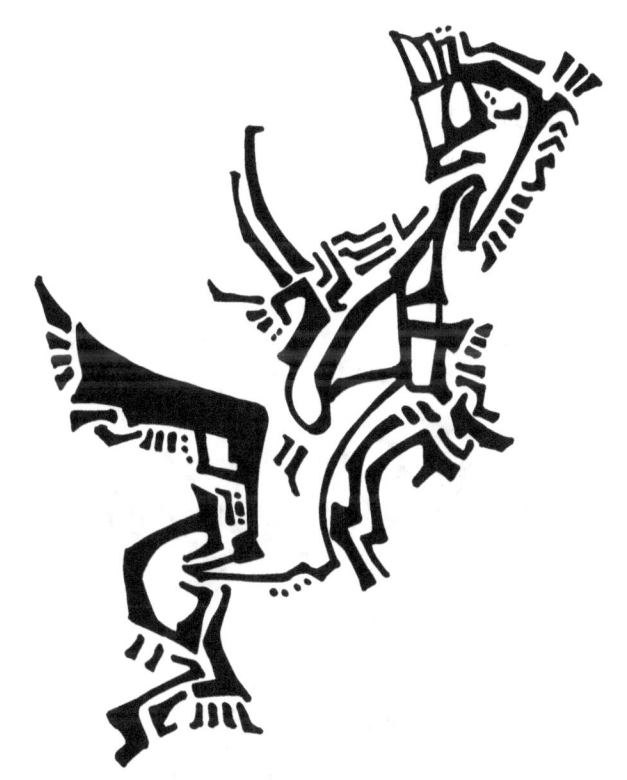

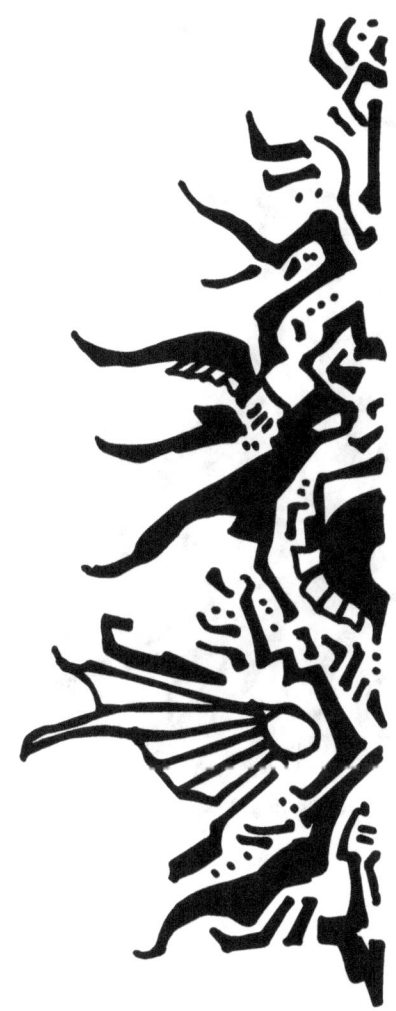

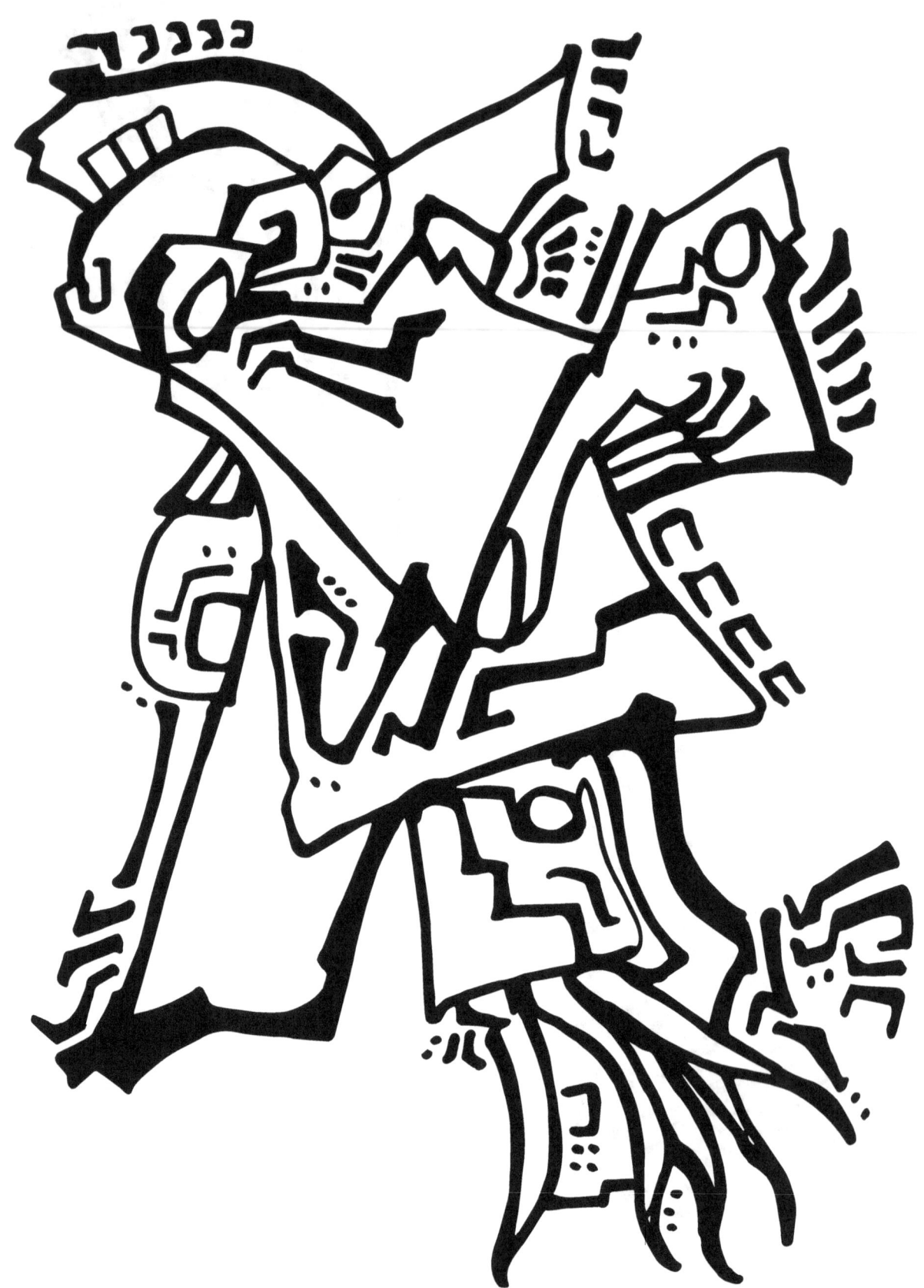

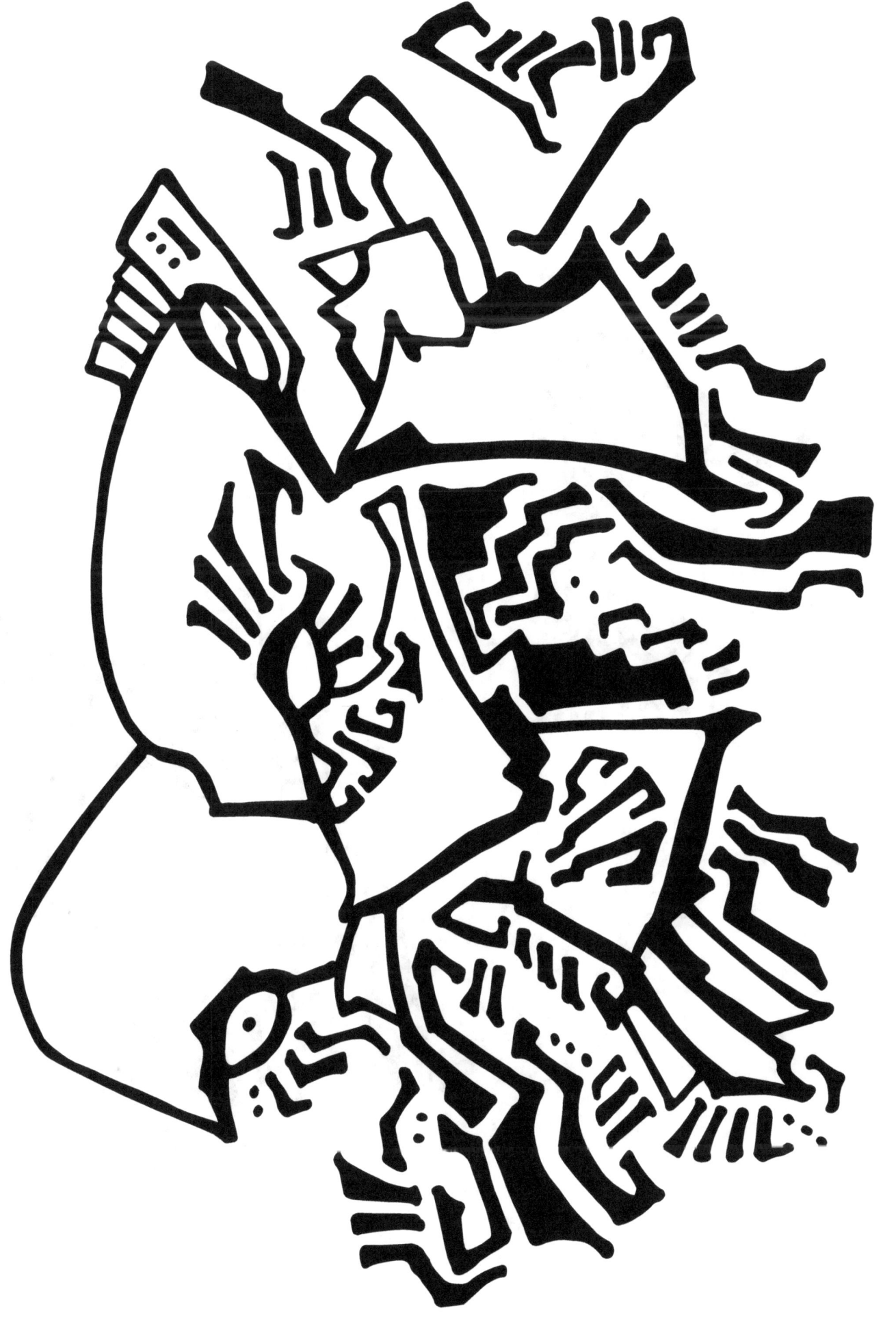

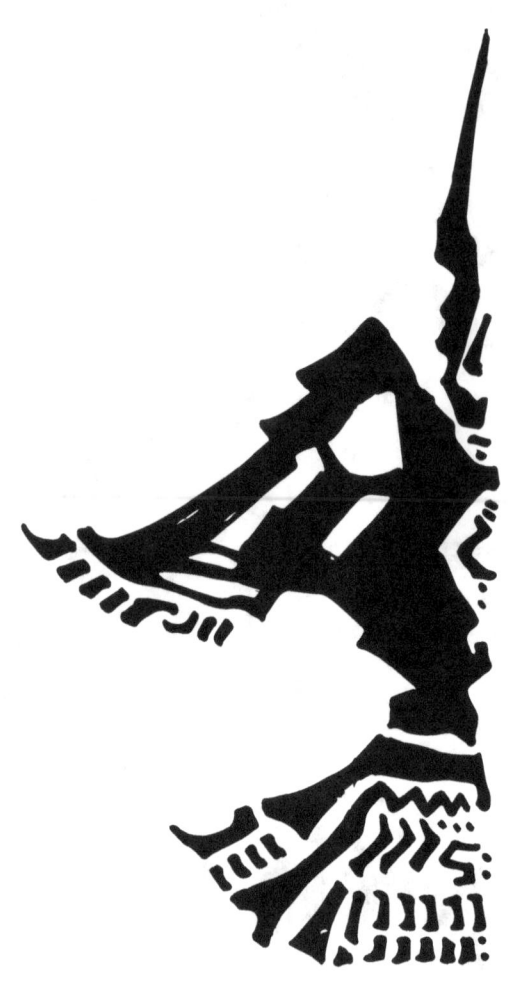

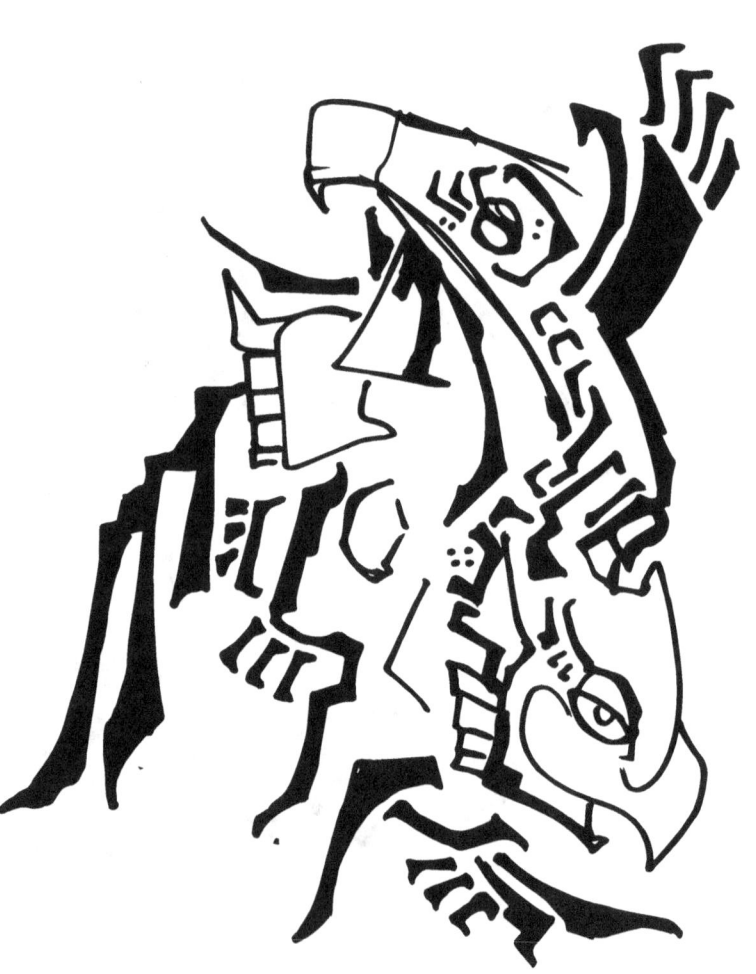

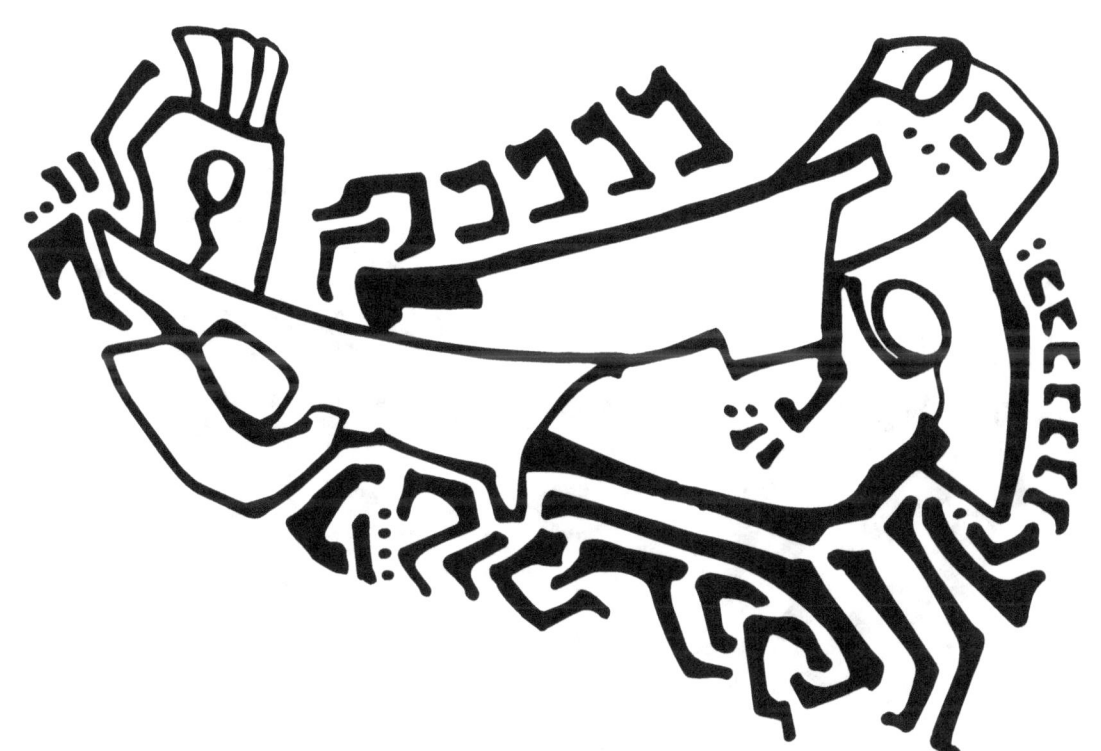

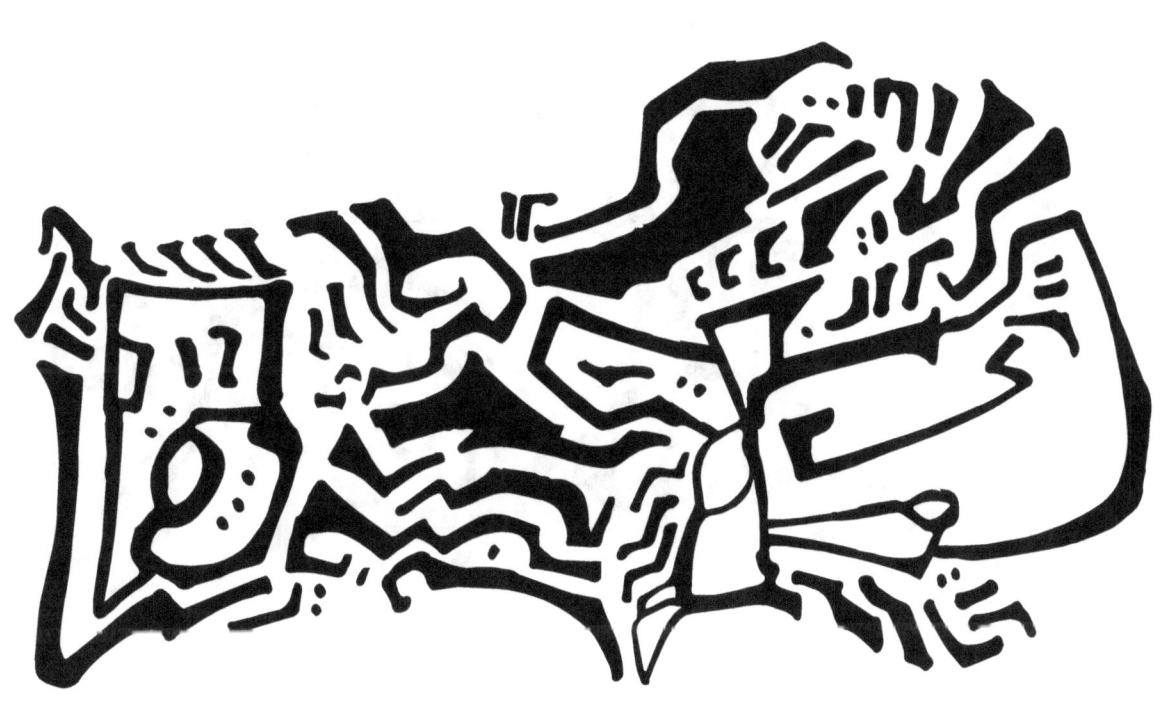

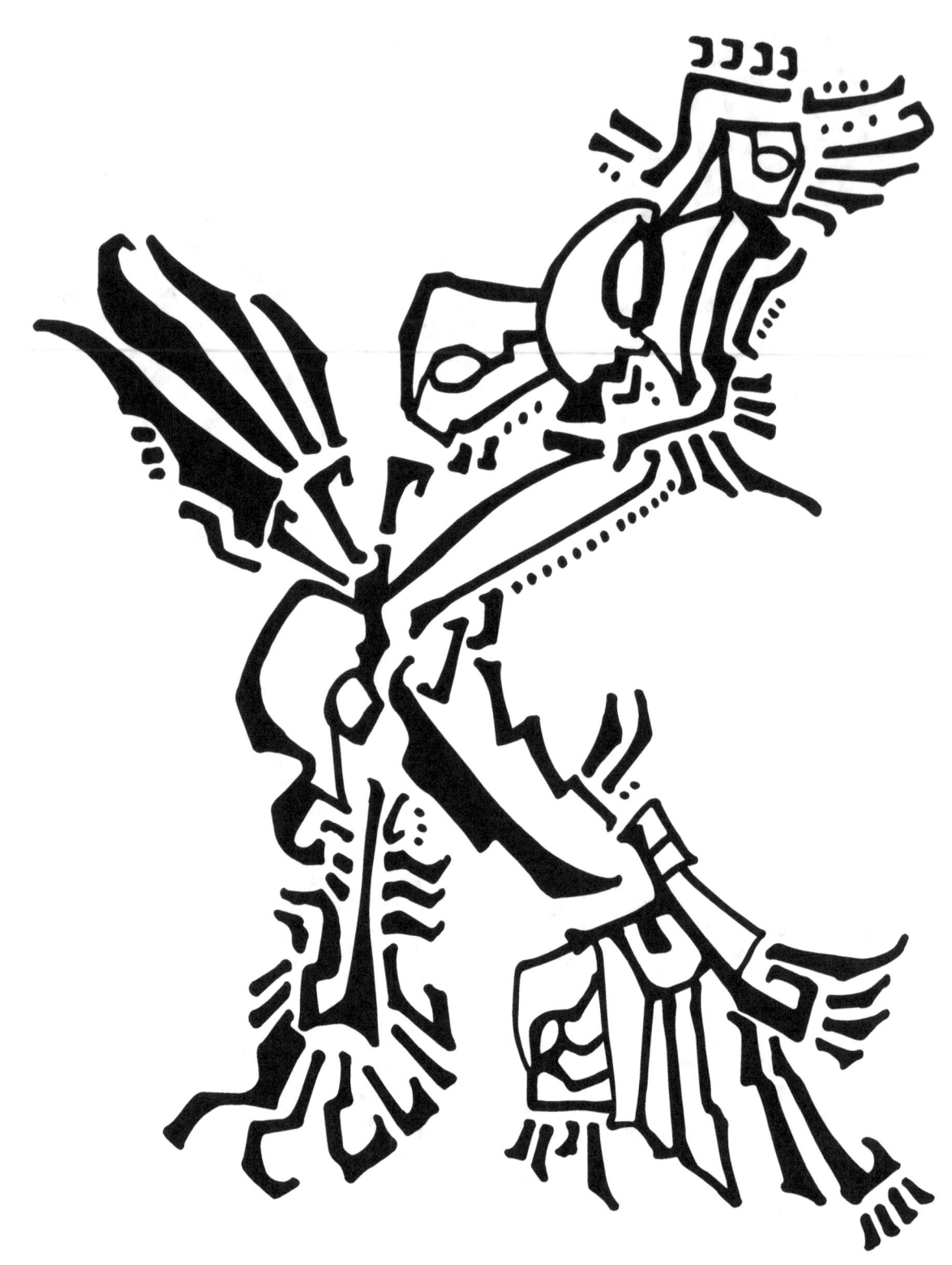

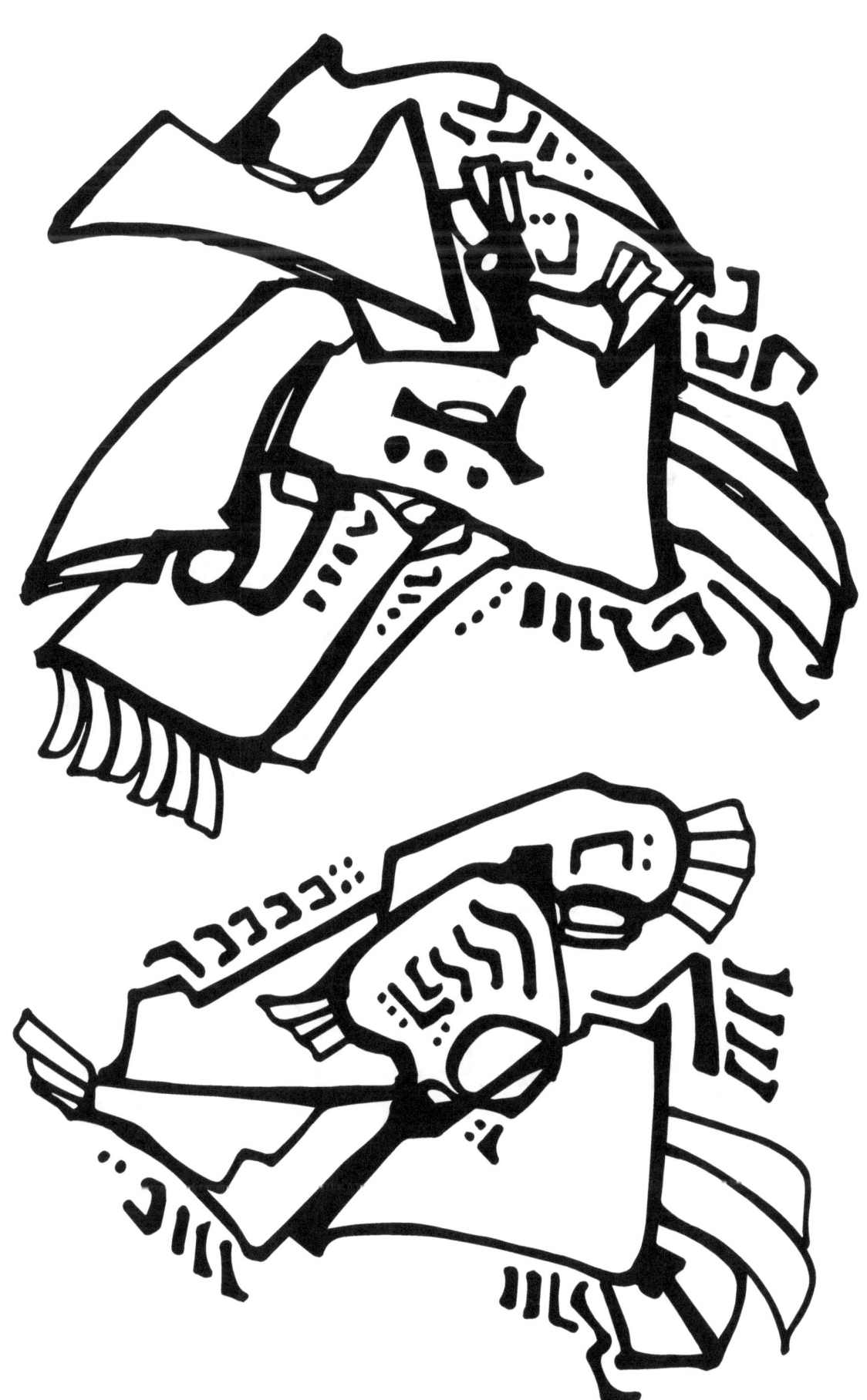

To All My Relations
Black Red Yellow White
and Everything Inbetween
In all corners of the universe
Tlazocamati

www.ingramcontent.com/pod-product-compliance
Lightning Source LLC
Chambersburg PA
CBHW081303170526
45165CB00011B/3390